JOHN UPDIKE

Modern Critical Views

These and other titles in preparation

Modern Critical Views

JOHN UPDIKE

Edited and with an introduction by
Harold Bloom
Sterling Professor of the Humanities
Yale University

CHELSEA HOUSE PUBLISHERS ◇ 1987
New York ◇ New Haven ◇ Philadelphia

© 1987 by Chelsea House Publishers, a division
of Chelsea House Educational Communications, Inc.,
  95 Madison Avenue, New York, NY 10016
  345 Whitney Avenue, New Haven, CT 06511
  5014 West Chester Pike, Edgemont, PA 19028

Introduction © 1987 by Harold Bloom

Printed and bound in the United States of America

∞ The paper used in this publication meets the minimum
requirements of the American National Standard for Permanence of
Paper for Printed Library Materials, Z39.48-1984.

Library of Congress Cataloging-in-Publication Data
John Updike.
    (Modern critical views)
    Bibliography: p.
    Includes index.
    Contents: The private vice of John Updike / John W.
Aldridge—John Updike / Richard H. Rupp—Post-pill
paradise lost / David Lodge—[etc.]
    1. Updike, John—Criticism and interpretation.
[1. Updike, John—Criticism and interpretation.
2. American literature—Criticism and interpretation]
I. Bloom, Harold.   II. Series.
PS3571.P4Z73   1987   813'.54   86–29971
ISBN 0–87754–717–3 (alk. paper)

Contents

Editor's Note

This book gathers together a representative selection of the best criticism devoted to the fiction of John Updike. The critical essays are reprinted in the chronological order of their original publication. I am grateful to Daniel Klotz for his erudite aid in editing this volume.

My introduction centers upon *The Witches of Eastwick*, finding in it a certain Updikean ambivalence towards his own moral and theological allegiances. John W. Aldridge begins the chronological sequence of criticism with a very negative overview of Updike that starts from a consideration of his minor novel, *Of the Farm*. In a more positive survey, also starting from *Of the Farm*, Richard H. Rupp compares Updike to John Cheever: two "ceremonial stylists" who make style a mode of withstanding the pressures of contemporary American life.

David Lodge, analyzing Updike's most notorious book, *Couples*, finds elements in it that remind him of Hawthorne, and defends the book as a serious work to which reviewers have been unfair. In a survey of Updike through *Couples*, Tony Tanner reads the novelist's argument as a dialectic of societal entropy and writerly subversion. The novelist Joyce Carol Oates, in a wide-ranging essay, praises Updike for his willingness to fight free of all perspectives, his own included.

In a fiercely feminist polemic, Mary Allen declares that "aside from lovemaking and childbearing, there is almost nothing for Updike's women to do," a judgment made before *The Witches of Eastwick*, which adds various deviltries to the female potential. *The Centaur*, one of Updike's major achievements, is studied by James M. Mellard as an elegiac celebration of the image of the father. Updike's short stories are analyzed by Jane Barnes as dark visions of family life in America.

Cynthia Ozick, novelist and story-writer, genially but sharply counters Updike's sharp and genial satire of the American Jewish novelist as his Bech. In this book's final essay, Donald J. Greiner considers Updike's most surprising novel, *The Coup*, which transfers his characteristic obsessions with belief in a secular society to the stormy world of contemporary Africa.

Introduction

John Updike, perhaps the most considerable stylist among the writers of fiction in his American generation, is one of a group of contemporary novelists who are somewhat victimized aesthetically by their conventional religious yearnings. His is the Protestant case that complements the Jewish instance of Cynthia Ozick and the Catholic example of Walker Percy. Piety, hardly an imaginative virtue in itself, becomes polemical in these authors, and testifies unto us with considerable tendentiousness, belatedness, and a kind of supernatural smugness that allows Updike to say "the natural is a pit of horror" and "one has nothing but the ancient assertions of Christianity to give one the will to act." As confessions of a particular personality, these have their poignance, but they neither enhance the narrative voices of Updike's fiction nor do they acquire any authority from Updike's prowess as a storyteller.

The three *Rabbit* novels are Updike's most characteristic achievement, but they scarcely sustain rereading, at least in my experience. Updike is certainly a representative novelist: of his time, his place, his society. He may seem, in another generation, to have been of the stature of John P. Marquand and John O'Hara, considerable craftsmen, who left us a single remarkable book each, in *H. M. Pulham, Esquire* and *Appointment in Samarra*, respectively. In my experience of reading Updike, that book is *The Witches of Eastwick*. I remember reading it, with fascination and disgust, when it came out two years ago (1984), and rereading it now has renewed both reactions. Whatever its final place among American novels, *The Witches of Eastwick* seems to me the unique book where Updike's religious polemic and his imagination of the natural otherness of particular human lives come into productive conflict. The conflict is pervasive in the *Rabbit* books and in *Couples*, but is obscured both by Updike's satire against those who seek transcendence through sexual relations and by his own lingering obsessions with that hopeless quest. *The Witches of Eastwick* is beyond satire; here distaste has turned into horror, and the antagonist is located in three natural

1

women who happen to be three highly dangerous witches, and two of them all the more charmingly human thereby.

Alexandra and Sukie are Updike's winsome and winning witches; Jane, more purely malevolent, is much less interesting, whether to Updike or to us. Three witches, as is traditional; the Devil, here Van Horne; the Devil's bride, poor Jenny;—that is all Updike needs as figures in his beautifully economical narrative. Though Van Horne is a failure in representation, and Jane and Jenny only limited successes, Alexandra and Sukie are so wonderfully rendered that Updike's book cannot fail. Alexandra, subtly Updike's favorite, is likeliest to enchant the male reader (myself as one) while Sukie perhaps pleases women readers more. Margaret Atwood, charmed by Updike's witches, commended them for their energy. I think that is accurate, and centers the novel's achievement; Updike has never lacked liveliness, but authentic exuberance or narrative gusto has not been one of his vivid strengths. *The Witches of Eastwick* is engagingly half-mad with a storyteller's exuberance, and Updike persuades me, possibly against his own intentions, that he loves Alexandra better even than Rabbit Angstrom.

Alexandra is darkly dominated by her fear of cancer, partly a literal fear and partly a metaphor for the vitalist's sense that nature always will betray the heart that loved her. A sculptor, Alexandra is best revealed by her works:

> Her figurines were in a sense primitive. Sukie or was it Jane had dubbed them her "bubbies"—chunky female bodies four or five inches long, often faceless and without feet, coiled or bent in recumbent positions and heavier than expected when held in the hand. People seemed to find them comforting and took them away from the shops, in a steady, sneaking trickle that intensified in the summer but was there even in January. Alexandra sculpted their naked forms, stabbing with the toothpick for a navel and never failing to provide a nicked hint of the vulval cleft, in protest against the false smoothness there of the dolls she had played with as a girl; then she painted clothes on them, sometimes pastel bathing suits, sometimes impossibly clinging gowns patterned in polka dots or asterisks or wavy cartoon-ocean stripes. No two were quite alike, though all were sisters. Her procedure was dictated by the feeling that as clothes were put on each morning over our nakedness, so they should be painted upon rather than carved onto these primal bodies of rounded soft clay. She baked them two dozen at a time in a little electric Swedish kiln kept in a workroom off her kitchen, an unfinished room but with a wood floor, unlike the next room, a dirt-floored storage space

where old flowerpots and lawn rakes, hoes and Wellington boots and pruning shears were kept. Self-taught, Alexandra had been at sculpture for five years—since before the divorce, to which it, like most manifestations of her blossoming selfhood, had contributed. Her children, especially Marcy, but Ben and little Eric too, hated the bubbies, thought them indecent, and once in their agony of embarrassment had shattered a batch that was cooling; but now they were reconciled, as if to defective siblings. Children are of a clay that to an extent remains soft, though irremediable twists show up in their mouths and a glaze of avoidance hardens in their eyes.

This grand paragraph, one of Updike's craftiest, ends with a sentence beyond praise, one of these sentences that makes me wonder sadly why so superb a stylist has not, in his work, attained to a more Jamesian eminence. The penultimate sentence is scarcely less powerful, with its reverberating conclusion: "but now they were reconciled, as if to defective siblings." The "bubbies" are representations at once of Alexandra's breasts and of her babies, and she forms them as a fierce critique of Yahweh's mode of creation of Adam, and even more of Yahweh's invidiously secondary creation of Eve from Adam's rib. Unable to breathe life into her figurines, Alexandra uses them to satirize the male vision of women as sensual objects: faceless, without the stance of feet, coiled snake-like, in recumbent postures, attired in beauty-contest bathing suits and impossibly clinging gowns.

Plump and stately, Alexandra is able to mock the male godhead also by creating, quite literally, her own thunderstorms. Her credo, nature's, is that there must always be sacrifice. Jane, the musician witch, is both more limited and more lethal, "with that burning insistence in her voice that an answer be provided forthwith, that a formula be produced with which to wedge life into place, to nail its secret down." The third witch, the journalist Sukie, is the most insouciant, bright and lithe, almost easy-going. All of them divorced, self-supporting, moving towards early middle age, the three inseparable friends form also a threesome of Sapphic lovers, liberated in all things and very much with a vengeance, since their unfortunate former spouses illustrate the power of these scorned women: Alexandra's former husband "rested in a high kitchen shelf in a jar, reduced to multi-colored dust, the cap screwed on tight," while "Jane Smart's ex, Sam, hung in the cellar of her ranch house among the dried herbs and simples and was occasionally sprinkled, a pinch at a time, into a philtre, for piquancy; and Sukie Rougemont had permanized hers in plastic and used him as a place mat."

Into the coven of these charmers comes the Devil as one Darryl Van Horne, a burly and expressionistic New Yorker who seems Updike's Bech, the Jewish novelist, gone demonic. Elements in Van Horne's personality suggest to me certain prominent novelists of Updike's generation, compounded into an unstable mixture. The Devil, poor fellow, is now past representation anyway, but Van Horne is a bore in any case. However, he captures all three witches, engages in hot-tub foursomes with them, expanded into five-person orgies when the beautiful young Jenny joins in.

The strength and the authentic horror of the novel come in its final section, when the three witches revenge themselves upon Jenny, merely for her marriage to Van Horne, by hexing her with a fatal cancer. Updike's surprising ambivalence towards his witches, who attract him at least as much as they repel him, emerges with a vivid power at their darkest moments. Only Alexandra, among them, is capable of feeling guilt at their murderous proclivities, and even Alexandra subsides into a pride at her own obscene accomplishment:

> Both her friends, with their veiled boasting of new lovers, were in Alexandra's eyes pictures of health—sleek and tan, growing strong on Jenny's death, pulling strength from it as from a man's body. Jane svelte and brown in her sandals and mini, and Sukie too wearing that summer glow Eastwick women got: terrycloth shorts that made her bottom look high and puffbally, and a peacocky shimmering dashiki her breasts twitched in a way that indicated no bra. Imagine being Sukie's age, thirty-three, and daring wear no bra! Ever since she was thirteen Alexandra had envied these pert-chested naturally slender girls, blithely eating and eating while her own spirit was saddled with stacks of flesh ready to topple into fat any time she took a second helping. Envious tears rose itching in her sinuses. Why was she mired so in life when a witch should dance, should skim? "We *can't* go on with it," she blurted out through the vodka as it tugged at the odd angles of the spindly little room. "We *must* undo the spell."
>
> "But how, dear?" Jane asked, flicking an ash from a red-filtered cigarette into the paisley-patterned dish from which Sukie had eaten all the pecans and then (Jane) sighing smokily, impatiently, through her nose, as if, having read Alexandra's mind, she had foreseen this tiresome outburst.
>
> "We *can't* just kill her like this," Alexandra went on, rather enjoying now the impression she must be making, of a blubbery troublesome big sister.
>
> "Why not?" Jane dryly asked. "We kill people in our minds all the time. We erase mistakes. We rearrange priorities."

"Maybe it's not our spell at all," Sukie offered. "Maybe we're being conceited. After all, she's in the hands of hospitals and doctors and they have all these instruments and counters and whatnot that don't lie."

"They *do* lie," Alexandra said. "All those scientific things lie. There *must* be a form we can follow to undo it," she pleaded. "If we all three *con*centrated."

"Count me out," Jane said. "Ceremonial magic really bores me, I've decided. It's too much like kindergarten. My whisk is still a mess from all that wax. And my children keep asking me what that thing in tinfoil was; they picked right up on it and I'm afraid are telling their friends. Don't forget, you two, I'm still hoping to get a church of my own, and a lot of gossip does *not* impress the good folk in a position to hire choirmasters."

"How can you be so callous?" Alexandra cried, deliciously feeling her emotions wash up against Sukie's slender antiques—the oval tilt-top table, the rush-seat three-legged Shaker chair—like a tidal wave carrying sticks of debris to the beach. "Don't you see how horrible it is? All she ever did was he asked her and she said yes, what else could she say?"

"I think it's rather amusing," Jane said, shaping her cigarette ash to a sharp point on the paisley saucer's brass edge. " 'Jenny died the other day,' " she added, as if quoting.

"Honey," Sukie said to Alexandra, "I'm honestly afraid it's out of our hands."

" 'Never was there such a lay,' " Jane was going on.

"You didn't do it, at worst you were the conduit. We all were."

" 'Youths and maidens, let us pray,' " quoted Jane, evidently concluding.

"We were just being *used* by the universe."

A certain pride of craft infected Alexandra. "You two couldn't have done it without me; I was *so* energetic, such a good organizer! It felt *won*derful, administering that horrible power!" Now it felt wonderful, her grief battering these walls and faces and things—the sea chest, the needlepoint stool, the thick lozenge panes—as if with massive pillows, the clouds of her agitation and remorse.

I can think of no contemporary except Updike who could write this virtuoso scene, with its bright intonations riding over a groundbass of malevolence. What is new, and unique, in Updike is his ability to extend an imaginative sympathy to his three witches. Perhaps their detailed verisimilitude is his cheerful testimony to his own sense of the reality of evil. Perhaps, as a man who loves and fears women, he has set down in one place his warding-off defense against a witchcraft that always has represented male fears of the power of female sexuality. For whatever cause, he has given us a memorable vision of a controlled male phantasmagoria that projects a sense of the radical otherness of all women.

Moralist as he may be, Updike is too fond of his witches, and too good an artist, to take revenge upon them. In a gracious coda, he breaks up the coven by marrying the ladies off, one by one, and then moving them out of Eastwick. The novel's concluding passage takes us into the elegy season, with a modulated pathos of an elegance extraordinary even in this meticulous and exquisite stylist:

> Jenny Gabriel lies with her parents under polished granite flush with the clipped grass in the new section of Cocumscussoc Cemetery. Chris, her brother and their son, has been, with his angelic visage and love of comic books, swallowed by the Sodom of New York. Lawyers now think that Darryl Van Horne was an assumed name. Yet several patents under that name do exist. Residents at the condo have reported mysterious crackling noises from some of the painted window sills, and wasps dead of shock. The facts of the financial imbroglio lie buried in vaults and drawers of old paperwork, silted over in even this short a span of time and of no great interest. What is of interest is what our minds retain, what our lives have given to the air. The witches are gone, vanished; we were just an interval in their lives, and they in ours. But as Sukie's blue-green ghost continues to haunt the sunstruck pavement, and Jane's black shape to flit past the moon, so the rumors of the days when they were solid among us, gorgeous and doing evil, have flavored the name of the town in the mouths of others, and for those of us who live here have left something oblong and invisible and exciting we do not understand. We meet it turning the corner where Hemlock meets Oak; it is there when we walk the beach in off-season and the Atlantic in its blackness mirrors the dense packed gray of the clouds: a scandal, life like smoke rising twisted into legend.

Updike studies the nostalgias here for his own Lady Macbeths and Madame Defarges, longing for "the days when they were solid among us, gorgeous and doing evil." Even here, at his most haunting, Updike comes a little short of his own literary tradition, the line that goes from Hawthorne through James and Conrad on to Fitzgerald and Hemingway. One listens for some reverberations in Updike's metaphors that would link his witches to Hawthorne's, or his sense of reality to the Henry James of the supernatural tales. But Updike evades every agonistic encounter with the force of the literary past. A minor novelist with a major style, he hovers always near a greatness he is too shrewd or too diffident to risk. He rarely fails, but nothing is got for nothing, and the American Sublime will never touch his pages.

JOHN W. ALDRIDGE

The Private Vice of John Updike

John Updike is one of those writers around whom we have generated a flamboyance of celebrity quite out of keeping with the value of anything they have so far written. In any reasonably discriminating age a young man of Mr. Updike's charming but limited gifts might expect to make his way in time to a position of some security in the second or just possibly the third rank of serious American novelists. But this is not a discriminating age. Hence, Mr. Updike has been able to arrive with ease at the very gates of first-rank status, and considering the size and fervor of his following, he should have no trouble at all getting in.

Just why this should be so it is extremely difficult to say, and the appearance of his new novel, *Of the Farm*, does not make it any easier. Mr. Updike has none of the attributes we conventionally associate with major literary talent. He does not have an interesting mind. He does not possess remarkable narrative gifts or a distinguished style. He does not create dynamic or colorful or deeply meaningful characters. He does not confront the reader with dramatic situations that bear the mark of an original or unique manner of seeing and responding to experience. He does not challenge the imagination or stimulate, shock, or educate it. In fact, one of the problems he poses for the critic is that he engages the imagination so little that one has real difficulty remembering his work long enough to think clearly about it. It has an annoying way of slipping out of the mind before one has had time to take hold of it, and of blending back into the commonplace and banal surfaces of reality, which are so monotonous a part

From *Time to Murder and Create: The Contemporary Novel in Crisis.* © 1966 by John W. Aldridge. David McKay, 1966.

of our daily awareness that the mind instinctively rejects them as not worth remembering.

Yet there can be no doubt that Mr. Updike does on occasion write well, although often with a kind of fussiness that makes one feel that the mere act of finding words that look attractive together on the page occupies entirely too much of his time and energy. There are, nonetheless, passages here and there in his novels of excellent description, mostly of landscapes, such as the long account in *The Centaur* of Peter Caldwell's early morning drive with his father into town, and Rabbit Angstrom's abortive flight down the highways in *Rabbit, Run*. There are also moments when Mr. Updike seems on the verge of becoming profound on the subject of the larger issues of life, love, death, and God. But then as a rule one senses that he does not, after all, know quite what he means to say and is hoping that sheer style will carry him over the difficulty. It is true, as Norman Mailer once remarked, that Mr. Updike tends to become confused when the action lapses, and so he cultivates his private vice: he *writes*. And the conviction grows on one that he *writes* a great deal too much of the time, and is too frequently ridden by the necessity to distract the reader's attention from the lapse by planting in his path yet another exquisitely described tree, shack, or billboard.

In his first three novels Mr. Updike should have been able to avoid these problems because he appeared to take great pains never to treat a subject for which a safe and secure precedent in literature did not exist. This, in fact, may well account for the high esteem in which he is currently held by so many people. For what he essentially accomplished in those novels was a skilled adaptation of the standard mannerisms and styles that have come over the years to be identified as belonging to the official serious modern mode of treating experience in fiction, and with which, therefore, many people felt comfortable, since they were relieved of the obligation to accommodate themselves to the new and unfamiliar and could sit back and enjoy being informed once again of what they already knew. Mr. Updike, in turn, was relieved of the obligation to think creatively and free to indulge his considerable talent for mimicking to perfection the best effects of other writers' originality.

It became apparent, however, that Mr. Updike shared with his admirers the handicap of being a good many years behind the times in his literary tastes. For example, his first novel, *The Poorhouse Fair*, was exactly the sort of book that back in the twenties and thirties would have represented an honest and rather radical confrontation of reality, but which by the middle fifties had become so respectably and fashionably "modern" that schools of writing were proudly turning it out by the dozens. It was a book essentially of style and terribly oblique and opaque and tinily inward observations of people, in which nothing discernible *happened*, but everything went on with dark throttled meaningfulness just beneath the surfaces, and faint ectoplasmic wisps of sensibility floated spookily about the page. In it Mr. Updike proved not only that he could work well in an outmoded convention, but that he could, if the need arose, *write* to cover a lapse of book-length duration.

Rabbit, Run, although brilliant in many of its superficial effects, was a botched attempt to explore certain important disorders of the modern will and spirit. It raised vital questions of freedom and responsibility that it answered vapidly. At just the point where it should have crystallized into meaning, it collapsed into a shambles of platitudes and stereotypes of alternative—rebellion versus conformity, the loving, passionate prostitute versus the dull, drunken, respectable wife—which nicely dramatized Mr. Updike's failure to come to fresh imaginative grips with his materials. *Rabbit, Run* might have been a deeply subversive book. Instead, it merely recapitulated subversive elements that had ceased with time and repeated literary usage to be subversive. It was spiced with a stale, High-Camp brand of *Angst* and a sexuality that had become merely a form of *writing* done with a different instrument, and, perhaps appropriately, the most viable possibility it appeared to hold out was that Rabbit probably ought to try very hard to make his peace with society, family, and God.

At the time he wrote *The Centaur*, Mr. Updike must have been alone among living writers in supposing that there could still be anything interesting or original to be done with the device of juxtaposing ancient myth and contemporary fact in fiction. Although T. S. Eliot did say after *Ulysses* was published that "Mr. Joyce is pursuing a method which others must pursue after him," one had assumed that the serious imitators of Joyce had all by now died of old age. But Mr. Updike, with his infallible instinct for the dated, apparently decided that there might be some kind of intellectual chic or status value to be found in carrying on the pursuit. He seems accordingly to have set out equipped only with the idea that all one needed to do was bring together some mythological figures and some contemporary characters and say that they were parallels, without troubling to create a dramatic situation in which they actually *became* parallels and therefore meaningful. Thus, he indicated in a thoughtfully provided epigraph and index that his story was a modern-dress reenactment of the legend of Chiron and Prometheus. But there was no reason to suppose that his protagonist, George Caldwell, was Chiron or anybody else but George Caldwell. His actions did not relate significantly or even coherently to those of the noblest of centaurs, and Chiron's shadow behind him contributed none of the comic irony that Odysseus contributed to Joyce's Bloom. It only served to muddle more completely a story that had no structure or point, and that Mr. Updike was clearly attempting to trick out in a bogus and antiquated literariness.

Of the Farm, although physically a small book, affords Mr. Updike a large opportunity to exercise his considerable powers of description. Never before has his private vice been so eloquently publicized. In fact, since he now has no rabbits or centaurs running for him, Mr. Updike is forced to describe pretty much all the time. There are descriptions of houses, barns, fields, flowers, trees, farm equipment, garden produce, and dogs. There is also a very good description of a tractor mowing a hay field.

The story itself is slight enough to have served as the basis for one of Mr. Updike's *New Yorker* stories, but even in the *New Yorker* it probably would have had to crescendo just a little, and this it does not do. It simply stops. It concerns the tensions that develop between a son and his ailing mother and the son's second wife when they all come together during a weekend down on the mother's farm. The mother, it seems, really preferred the first wife, although she appears not to care very much for either wife, and she certainly does not care for her son, who is full of bitterness toward her. At any rate, this drama, which develops at about the speed of creeping crab grass, is interrupted at intervals to give Mr. Updike an opportunity to make sure that the reader has the scene firmly in mind. And just to make doubly sure, he inserts some further descriptions of details he failed to mention earlier, such as the appearance of a church where the mother and son attend service, a supermarket where they go to buy groceries, and the new wife's excellent thighs in a bikini.

But these digressions come to seem more and more pleasant and necessary as the novel proceeds. Indeed, one begins to feel almost grateful to the action for lapsing, for at least the interludes of scenic commercials introduce subjects about whose reality there can be no question. They have what Henry James would have called "density of specification," and finally they justify their existence in the novel by creating a happy heterogeneity of clutter into which the domestic tensions sink and finally disappear. It seems after a while that all the difficulties we have watched developing among the characters become assimilated into the bucolic setting, that a satisfactory mediation has been achieved between the petty troubles of men and women and the eternal harmonies of nature, so that what at first promised to be a disturbing book turns out to be an essentially placid and contented book.

The effect of the book is finally so agreeable and reassuring that one feels that it would be almost offensive to speak of its possible meaning. Yet meaning it most assuredly has. In fact, one can even say that it has a message, although as is the case with all Mr. Updike's books, it does not yield up this message easily. Every effort is made to keep it subtle, and the reader is constantly being put off its track by various cagey covering movements of Mr. Updike's. But one can, after some searching, ferret it out from its hiding place behind the rich, beautiful scenery of the descriptive prose. I suppose there is no harm in revealing it, since it is bound to become common knowledge very soon. Mr. Updike has nothing to say.

RICHARD H. RUPP

John Updike:
Style in Search of a Center

We in America need ceremonies, is I suppose, sailor, the point of what I have written.

Like Cheever, John Updike is concerned with ceremonial style. Though neither writer can project a sustained festive action, each man tries to make style carry the burden of a ceremonial attitude toward life. Updike's ceremony is different from Cheever's, however, in some important ways: first, Cheever's ceremonial style is founded on social and religious certitudes, whereas Updike's style is not. Second, Cheever's ceremonies are generally social and lighthearted, whereas Updike's are solitary and solemn. Compare Updike's George Caldwell and Leander Wapshot, for instance: Caldwell is a master of ceremony, a noble agonist largely detached from the world around him. Leander is very much involved in the vicissitudes of life and is more often than not the butt of its jokes. Third, Updike's style is highly self-conscious, whereas Cheever's is not. Cheever falls in and out of narrative commentary with careless ease; Updike's narrator is more solemn. As a result Updike's style circles relentlessly on the circumference of experience, seeking entry into its center.

I do not wish to imply that Updike is merely superficial. He simply has no starting point for natural ceremonies, no St. Botolphs. If Cheever's problem is finding a substitute world with a coherence and a vitality for the world of St. Botolphs, Updike's problem is believing that such a world can exist. Consequently, ceremony is dependent on Updike's world of the moment, upon the

---

From *Celebration in Postwar American Fiction 1945–1967.* © 1970 by the University of Miami Press.

15

shifting sensibility of the author. The protagonist in his stories must find restorative ceremonies on his own.

Updike's style bears the double burden of making a world and making it festive. At its worst the feast is merely verbal, an indulgence of poetic epiphanies bursting like Roman candles in the summer sky. At its best, however, in stories like "Packed Dirt," "The Blessed Man of Boston," and *The Centaur*, the private feast becomes a joyful public action, liberating the isolated sensibility in a communal song of love. At such times style finds its center.

The most obvious characteristic of Updike's style is his exhaustive exploration of minute physical detail. Even in his first collection, *The Same Door* (1959), the scene is microscopic. Take the following passage, for instance:

> He was perfect: the medium-short dry-combed hair, the unimpeachable brown suit, the buttonless collar, the genially dragged vowels, the little edges of efficiency bracing the consonants. Some traces of the scholarship-bothered freshman from Hampton (Md.) High School who had come down to the *Quaff* on Candidates' Night with an armful of framed sports cartoons remained—the not smoking, the tucked-in chin and the attendant uplook of the boyishly lucid eyes, and the skin allergy that placed on the flank of each jaw a constellation of red dots.
>
> ("Who Made Yellow Roses Yellow?")

The cadences fall smoothly. The catalogue of physical traits is complete, down to the shape of the rash on Clayton's jaws. Such catalogues, rhythmic phrasing, proper nouns, and brand names are all marks of Updike's style. But their primary function is to establish the writer's authority: the story itself is secondary. This is a new look at experience, a new voice speaking. We remember the voice far longer than the story.

The narrative voice is largely concerned with ways of feeling. The characters in Updike's first collection of stories are young, sensitive, and intelligent people. More often than not, Updike juxtaposes them against a vaguely hostile urban environment. Obliquely, the stories chronicle integrity, honesty, and the confrontation of experience.

"Toward Evening" tells of a young married man, Rafe, returning home after work with a mobile for his daughter. Half-dreaming, he is aroused by the sight of a beautiful redhead at the back of the bus, then by a mulatto. The bus, the two women, and Rafe's dreams are juxtaposed against his apartment, wife, and baby girl. At the end of the story, Rafe has finished his favorite meal, which, like the clumsy mobile for the baby, is vaguely disappointing. Husband and wife are balanced against each other and against the outside world in a silent struggle to find the right way. Their life is dominated by a huge Spry sign, white and red, blinking through their window from the Jersey shore. In a brisk rondo, Updike explains how the sign got there, and the account is a perfect example of the unfestive, commercialized existence that Rafe can feel but cannot explain to Alice. Without comment, Updike ends the story.

A second story presents a small-town version of this conflict, "Ace in the Hole"—a story that is the germ of *Rabbit, Run*. The setting is Olinger, an eastern Pennsylvania town near the Dutch country. (Olinger is also the setting for *The Centaur* and several of the stories in *Pigeon Feathers*.) Ace Anderson is more boy than man. An ex-basketball star in high school, Ace has just been fired from his job parking cars. He stops at his mother's to pick up his daughter and ponders how to explain the firing to his wife. He doesn't explain, though. Flipping on the radio, he seizes his wife and dances away from his problems, stilling her protests in their dance. "The music ate through his skin and mixed with the nerves and small veins; he seemed to be great again, and all the other kids were around them, in a ring, clapping time."

Ace's escape is an uneasy compromise between athletic pride and responsibility to his wife and daughter. For the moment he has dodged his crisis, but the difficulty remains: Ace has no idea of what to do. Needing contact with others but unable to make it, he plays the radio and the television incessantly. In these stories of conflict between the mechanized present and the family, dancing is only an evasion.

Though brilliant, the stories in *The Same Door* do not show the connection between the periphery of experience and the center. The style catches only the outside of things, the shell of the corporate experience we all have in being twentieth-century Americans. The inside, the characters' capacity to connect feeling and form, is missing. The range of emotional response, furthermore, is quite limited. Updike's self-conscious characters guard themselves from each other, and from the reader. At worst the style leaves only an empty husk. At best it reveals characters who are potentially interesting. One does not remember them by name, only collectively—the young husband, the student abroad, the long-suffering wife.

The second collection of stories, *Pigeon Feathers* (1962), shows some improvements in the attempt to make the internal connection. Most impressive technically is Updike's montage effect, achieved by a juxtaposition of entirely separate scenes in the same story. Hints of such a development have appeared earlier, in "Toward Evening," for example. As Rafe moved from bus to apartment to Spry sign, the overlapping scenes commented silently on each other.

In *Pigeon Feathers*, the montage technique is more evident. Three stories especially demonstrate the effect. The first of them, "Home," portrays Robert's return from England with his wife and child. He plans to spend July with his parents before going to teach mathematics at a girls' college. Robert's father, an amiable Pennsylvania high school teacher—one of many in Updike's fiction—understands almost nothing of modern ways. His simple reactions to situations are open and genuine; they embarrass his sophisticated son.

The first half of the story tells of the many small corruptions involved in this homecoming—corruptions of feeling, loyalty, and speech. Robert's values are always in motion, it seems; but his father gives them substance in an unexpected encounter. The second half of the story recounts his only triumph, that won by default over a belligerent Pennsylvania Dutchman they pass on the highway. The Dutchman pursues them down the road; the father pulls off on the shoulder and stops. The Dutchman also stops, ahead of them, and trots back to them howling obscenities. The father gets out to speak to him, but the Dutchman, suddenly afraid, turns and runs back to his car. Robert's father is ignorant of his triumph: "That man had something to say to me and I wanted to hear what it was." Puzzled, he gets back into the ancient Plymouth and begins to drive on.

The two parts of the story move Robert to a feeling of joy. In the person of his father, home once more becomes real for him. His father's awkwardness, his hopeless innocence, his openness to the world make him genuine. He symbolizes the ceremonies of the land, the rural Pennsylvania of his son's youth, unchanged by scholarship and sophistication.

Furthermore, the father is a memorable character. He has much in common with the grandmother in "The Blessed Man of Boston, My Grandmother's Thimble, and Fanning Island," and with Mr. Kern, the dying father in "Packed Dirt, Churchgoing, A Dying Cat, A Traded Car." Each story reveals a young man's reaction to his inheritance—a ceremonial reaction. The three older figures, gauche and out of touch, represent tradition and a coherent life. For the young they are a source of strength and self-definition.

"The Blessed Man" juxtaposes three characters: a smiling Chinaman, serene amidst the mob scrambling out of Fenway Park; the narrator's grandmother, who had clung to life tenaciously and left him her only possession, a silver thimble; and a nameless Polynesian, the last of his tribe, writing a journal on Fanning Island. Each character is the custodian of a tradition that is handed down to the narrator and then to us. Writing the story thus celebrates filial piety, a sense of the goodness and continuity of experience. The reader, like the narrator, must make the leap of faith:

> This is the outline; but it would be the days, the evocation of the
> days . . . the green days. The tasks, the grass, the weather, the shades
> of sea and air. Just as a piece of turf torn from a meadow becomes a

gloria when drawn by Dürer. Details. Details are the giant's fingers. He seizes the stick and strips the bark and shows, burning beneath, the moist white wood of joy. For I thought that this story, fully told, would become without my willing it a happy story, a story full of joy; had my powers been greater, we would know. As it is, you, like me, must take it on faith.

Style here serves Updike well: unconnected experiences move the narrator to a leap of affirmation, a commitment to tradition. At the end of "Packed Dirt," for instance, the narrator equates the car he is trading in with his father's death, and it makes him glad:

> Any day now we'll trade it in; we are just waiting for the phone to ring. I know how it will be. My father traded in many cars. It happens so cleanly, before you expect it. He would drive off in the old car up the dirt road exactly as usual and when he returned the car would be new, and the old was gone, gone, utterly dissolved back into the mineral world from which it was conjured, dismissed without a blessing, a kiss, a testament, or any ceremony of farewell. We in America need ceremonies, is I suppose, sailor, the point of what I have written.

These three stories, probably the best in the collection (though "Pigeon Feathers" and "The Doctor's Wife" are fine and moving), stress a common theme, revealed through a common technique: We need ceremonies, for they keep us in touch with the familial past, the only true source of strength and identity. The montage technique demonstrates the personal reconstruction of experience by the narrator. He finds his center in a past refashioned for present needs, present living.

Other stylistic experiments in *Pigeon Feathers*, however, are not so successful. One story, "Dear Alexandros," uses the epistolary style in a manner reminiscent of "For Esmé—With Love and Squalor." But Updike's story lacks the honest feeling of Salinger's. He substitutes situational irony for Salinger's compassion. While Updike avoids sentimentality (which he charges Salinger with elsewhere), he substitutes less feeling altogether. The contrast between the past happiness and the present misery of the now-divorced American father who is answering the letter from an innocent Greek orphan whom he and his wife had sponsored in the early years of their marriage is simply too pat.

Another stylistic dead end is "Archangel," a story told literally from the angelic viewpoint. It too is a ceremonial story, like "Packed Dirt," for it catalogues the various pleasures of angelic life. Heaped up with dazzling metaphors and unusual yokings, the story is too ingenious to manifest a human ceremony—but that may be its point.

Two other stories exemplify what we might call baroque style: "Wife-Wooing" and "Lifeguard." In each story Updike is experimenting with unreliable narrators. Each narrator takes himself and his situation far too seriously, indulging his capacity to formulate sense impressions. The narrator in "Wife-Wooing" defines the import of his experience in a way which is simply silly: "Monday's wan breakfast light bleaches you blotchily, drains the goodness from your thickness, makes the bathrobe a limp stained tube flapping disconsolately, exposing sallow decolletage." These stories are exercises for Updike, self-reminders to avoid the excesses that they portray.

On the whole, the experiments in *Pigeon Feathers* meet with mixed success. Updike writes best of simple people; but in this collection he does not always close the gap between style and emotion, between the outside and the inside.

The four novels represent a clearer development in Updike's style. The first of them, *The Poorhouse Fair* (1958), is the simplest. The story takes place in a state house for the aged toward the end of our century. Its subject is freedom; its theme is that freedom is the property of those who preserve their identity amidst the indignities of life.

The poorhouse itself is an anomaly. Those who have power, the administrators, are imprisoned in a struggle for supremacy. The aged residents, on the other hand, are variously free. Certain of themselves, they can ignore the machinations of those in charge. The best of them have a sense of tradition and ceremony based on an ingrained sense of order. Within the walls of an institution supposedly depriving them of their freedom, they find it anew.

Their strength is built on a ceremonial sense of life. Despite a rainstorm, they put up booths. Unflappable, they sit soaking on the porch, waiting for the band to play. The band has always played at the fair; it must play now, and it does. Updike's point, however, is that ceremony is dying with these aged poor. When they go, they will take the ceremonial sense of life with them.

The novel is anti-utopian satire. As a symbol of the welfare state, the poorhouse is a prison; its annual fair is the only sign of a corporate life better than the daily isolation. Thus the fair is a curious relic of the ordered past imbedded in the fabric of the disordered present. For John Updike, as for Edward Albee, the American Dream ends in banalities and obscenities.

Conner, the prefect, is the composite organization man; he accepts the dehumanization of the aged residents with glib sociological formulas. Updike's style, especially when Conner is the subject, becomes gray and bureaucratic:

> At any rate there was nothing to do but persevere in his work. He would not, unlike Mendelssohn, be a poorhouse prefect forever. In

another year or two, if his progress here continued to look impressive on paper—the two most important statistics were the yield from the farm and the longevity of the inmates—he would be moved up, perhaps into a State Health Service Council. He expected association with scientists to be pleasanter, more suited to his gifts and to the quality of his dedication. Still, he prized a useful over a pleasant life. Wherever I can serve, he told himself.

The other end of the stylistic spectrum is evidenced by Gregg, who leads a hooting mob of aged residents in stoning Conner: "Son of a bitch of a cat-killer, brave bastard run your a. h. off." Conner recovers from the indignity and tries to forget it. But the style indicates the problem: the world of the future vitiates all ceremony, all tradition. In its swing from institutional prose to invective, Updike's style describes a world without proportion, that yardstick of civilized society.

Despite the clean bite of his irony, Updike's lyricism is the dominant quality of the style. He has a fine sense of place in this novel. The pages describing western New Jersey and the poorhouse lawn after a rain are the most poetic in the novel. This is Updike's country; he has found a context for tradition that he will develop more fully and more ambitiously in his later novels.

In a sense *Rabbit, Run* (1960) poses a question which *The Centaur* answers: how does a man love? Implicit in the question is a context for love and for freedom. In *Rabbit, Run* that context is the rootless present, in which family, church, and the individual are sterile. In *The Centaur* that present is richly permeated with the past and its multiple traditions.

Running is the basic metaphor of Updike's second novel. Rabbit Angstrom runs through all the certitudes of his life. He was once a high school basketball star but is now a sometime used-car salesman. He once loved his wife, but in a fit of disgust at her stupidity he leaves her for another girl. One by one, Rabbit's certitudes collapse: belief in God, belief in love, belief in his own beauty.

Rabbit's certitudes are based on feeling. In order to act, he must feel that what he does is right. Right feeling becomes an obsession with Rabbit; he wants everything he does to feel right to him. But as his problems increase, feeling ceases to guide him.

He leaves Ruth, his girlfriend, when his wife, Janice, has their second baby: he feels his place is with his wife. He leaves Janice a second time after she refuses him, still tender from the stitches of childbirth: he feels that his marital rights have been abrogated. He flies to Ruth once again, after Janice drunkenly drowns the baby in the bathtub. This time feeling cannot guide him: Ruth is pregnant. He must choose.

"Please have the baby," he says. "You got to have it."
"Why? Why do you *care*?"

"I don't know. I don't know any of these answers. All I know is what feels right. You feel right to me. Sometimes Janice used to. Sometimes nothing does."

"Who cares? That's the thing. Who cares *what* you feel?"

"I don't know," he says again.

In truth, Rabbit does not know. He reacts, he moves. Movement has always carried him through, and he hopes it will continue to do so. The novel opens with an alley scrimmage, where Rabbit, six feet three and twenty-six, drives and fakes past the grade school kids. Memories of past successes crowd about him thereafter. The motions of basketball merge in his memory with the motions of sex. In motion he finds victory, upon which he builds his identity.

Two extended motions reflect Rabbit's character. The first, immediately after his initial break with Janice, is a restless all-night drive from Brewer (Reading) to West Virginia and back. Updike's style fits itself around Rabbit's nervous vibrations like a glove here:

> He drives through Frederick, a discouraging town because an hour back he had thought he had reached Frederick when it was really Westminster. He picks up 340. The road unravels with infuriating slowness, its black wall wearilessly rising in front of his headlights no matter how they twist. The tar sucks his tires. . . . He grinds his foot down as if to squash this snake of a road, and nearly loses the car on a curve, as the two right wheels fall captive to the dirt shoulder. He brings them back but keeps the speedometer needle leaning to the right.

Through all this we get a sense of Rabbit's feeling: blind panic guided only by motor reflexes. The style chronicles the exact stimulus and the precise shade of response on Rabbit's part.

Rabbit, Run is a powerful novel, but it overwhelms its hero. Dependent upon appropriate feeling, Rabbit can only respond to his situation—he cannot initiate action. His ceremonies are basketball and sex. He knows his role as celebrant in each area. Once the demands of responsible adulthood impinge upon him, he can no longer be a hero. The age of innocent heroism is past, leaving Rabbit with no role to play. The plot neatly cancels his attempts to feel his way: modern life does not allow feeling. It confronts him with the dilemma of Janice and her dead baby versus a pregnant Ruth. Feeling can carry him no further.

The conclusion gives us the second extended motion, Rabbit's flight from the cemetery. Blindly he stumbles through the undergrowth. Branches catch at him, tearing his shirt. He pauses in his flight only to plead with Ruth to have the baby and then stumbles on, at last alone. "His hands lift of their own and he feels the wind on his ears even before, his heels hitting heavily on the pavement at first but with an effortless gathering out of a kind of sweet panic growing lighter and quicker and quieter, he runs. Ah: runs. Runs."

Updike's style in *Rabbit, Run* projects powerful feelings: innocence, isolation, self-delusion, betrayal. His nostalgia for high school glories and uncomplicated sex comes through clearly, but the very power of such memories isolates him from what is happening to him at the moment. Updike plays the devil's advocate with Rabbit: the activities in which he excels, speed and sex, have no commercial value. As his nickname indicates, Rabbit can only run and breed. He does not know what is happening to him. He has an incorruptible innocence and a belief in his dignity as a person. But circumstances destroy him.

Updike has instilled most of urban man's frustrations into his hapless hero; the book is a kind of extended elegy for the child's view of life. Perhaps Rabbit *is* the representative modern man. But Rabbit is too much an indictment of the inhuman present and too little a character who lives in it.

Rabbit, Run exorcises the demons possessing its author. The style is a kind of weapon in his attack on the present. Religion is a special target of that attack. When Updike describes the impact of religion on Rabbit, who genuinely desires to repent and to believe, he either burlesques the institutions of religion through the insipid Reverend Eccles or else he cranks out a pat symbol of life without God: "Afraid, really afraid, he remembers what once consoled him by seeming to make a hole where he looked through into underlying brightness, and lifts his eyes to the church window. It is, because of church poverty or the late summer nights or just carelessness, unlit, a dark circle in a stone facade."

Our clearest view of Rabbit comes from Ruth, the most realized character in the novel. She sees his vitality, his pride, and his final defeat. Yet she is not the emotional center of the novel—he is. When he runs away from her at the end, he runs toward a self he will never reach, an ideal destroyed by his lust, his guilt, and the spiritual poverty of modern life.

Whatever our reservations about it, *Rabbit, Run* is a considerable advance for Updike. The relationship between Rabbit and the two women is well done. With both, Rabbit feels the need to be a husband and father. Yet he cannot accept his share in the drowning of his daughter. He wants to accept his role as the father of Ruth's baby, but he doesn't know how. *Rabbit, Run* simply inverts the situation of "The Blessed Man" and "Packed Dirt," but the values on which the emotion rests are the same: familial love and a sense of the past. They are simply unavailable for Rabbit Angstrom. Unable to resolve past and present, Rabbit runs.

The Centaur is a ceremonial statement of man's power to love and to order his experience in love. That ability is based on a dual nature. George Caldwell develops a center that Rabbit never found because he is at once a schoolteacher and a centaur, i.e., he is vitally involved in both past and present and can place present action in the widest possible context. One of the marvels of the novel is Updike's ability to render both natures without contradiction.

A chief means of rendering Caldwell is Updike's handling of point of view. Four chapters (1, 3, 9, and the epilogue) are told from Chiron's point of view. One chapter, 5, is told by the omniscient narrator and one, 7, by George Caldwell himself.

Second in importance to Caldwell-Chiron is his son Peter. The myth of the novel dramatizes the death of Chiron, who, wounded with a silver arrow, offers himself to Zeus as an expiation for the sin of Prometheus. In his own person, Peter expresses the love of life that his father tried to instill in him, Chiron's only real student.

In addition to point of view, the mythological parallels help to unite past and present. Thus we have Peter's girlfriend Penny (Pandora); Al Hummel, the garage man (Hephaestus); his promiscuous wife Vera (Venus); Zimmerman, the high school principal (Zeus); Pop Kramer, Caldwell's father-in-law (Kronos), etc. Tongue in cheek, Updike indexes all the parallels at the end of the novel.

One effect of the mythologizing is comedy; *The Centaur* is Updike's only comic novel. In a riotous class on the origins of man, the wounded Caldwell must contend with the seduction of two girls before his eyes, one by Zimmerman. The class meanwhile seethes with a desire to escape. Furiously racing the clock, Chiron-Caldwell ends his account on a note of incorrigible hope: "He opened his mouth; his very blood loathed the story he had told. 'One minute ago, flint-chipping, fire-kindling, death-foreseeing, a tragic animal appeared —' The buzzer rasped; halls rumbled throughout the vast building; faintness swooped at Caldwell but he held himself upright, having vowed to finish. '—called Man.' "

Caldwell's task is hopeless. Having met Mim Herzog (Hera) emerging mussed from Zimmerman's office, he expects to be fired. Moreover, he lives in constant knowledge of his coming death. But like Chiron, the wisest and gentlest of the untamed centaurs, Caldwell has a compulsion to teach anyway. Chapter 3 shows him at his best—Chiron now, teaching the sons and daughters of the gods: "Chiron inhaled; air like honey expanded the spaces of his chest; his students completed the centaur. They fleshed his wisdom with expectation. The wintry chaos of information within him, elicited into sunlight, was struck through with the young colors of optimism. Winter turned vernal." This is the past that George Caldwell brings to his biology classes at Olinger High School. Teaching is the ceremonial connection between Greek myth and contemporary life; it is a gesture of piety before God.

Chapter 3 works against chapter 1 in every way. Here Updike gives us the ideal teacher, ideal students, in an idyllic setting. The style itself shows significant changes. "The air like honey" expands in Chiron's breast. Abstract nouns, denoting the qualities of a state of life, abound—"wisdom, wintry chaos, optimism." Setting and character are eternal and transcendent.

Such marked contrasts in style continue throughout the book. At such times Updike celebrates his own liturgy, to use Michael Novak's term. Thus the mythological parallels have a significant purpose in the novel; they posit a belief in the old gods. In the elaborate catechesis with Venus in the girls' locker room, Chiron overcomes his own desire for the beautiful goddess and asserts his belief in the gods. To Chiron, "reality" is the joke. It is a travesty of the world that used to be—and through belief still is.

Technique serves Updike well in this task of reversing our notions of reality. Even-numbered chapters, told by Peter, give us the necessary filter of an awareness removed one degree from experience. Filial piety does not allow frequent access to Caldwell's mind, and never for any length of time. Thus Updike can use Peter as his spokesman and can mythologize the centaur-father. And in keeping the two apart, Updike can dramatize the common bond of nostalgia for a better time and place: Caldwell for Mt. Olympus, Peter for his childhood and his magical father.

More important, however, is the thematic importance of technique. Caldwell's spectacular failure to control the events of his life is a clue to the theme: his life for his son's. At the end we realize that the significance of the story is that Caldwell's love allows Peter to act. Peter realizes the sacrifice that Chiron has made for him, Prometheus. He feels inadequate to recompense his father for what he has done. His chapters are an elegiac tribute to his father's memory: "I am my father's son. In the late afternoons while the day hangs in distending light waiting to be punctured by the darkness that in arrows of shadow rides out from the tall buildings across the grid of streets, I remember my father and even picture—eyes milky with doubts, mustache indecisive and pale—his father before him, whom I never knew. Priest, teacher, artist: the classic degeneration."

The epilogue indicates that the sacrifice is acceptable: "Zeus had loved his old friend, and lifted him up, and set him among the stars as the constellation Sagittarius. Here, in the Zodiac, now above, now below the horizon, he assists in the regulation of our destinies, though in this latter time few living mortals cast their eyes respectfully toward Heaven, and fewer still sit as students to the stars."

Updike himself is such a student. In *The Centaur* he formulates rituals for connecting son and father, present and past. Like Mark Twain and Henry Adams before him, Updike has found a usable past. No matter that it is the most remote in human memory. It is usable, and offers at last a center, pulling all toward itself.

Throughout these three novels the ceremonies of existence depend upon the protagonist's ability to connect present experience with traditional attitudes and values. Ceremony is always a rite of connection for Updike: The poorhouse with its band, its homemade candy, and its patchwork quilts is a gesture toward the continuity of things; the vitiation of all ceremonies disconnects Rabbit from wife, home, and God; the filial pieties of George Caldwell and his son are a source of life and renewal for them. In each case the ceremonial action, whether anonymous (*The Poorhouse Fair*), inverted (*Rabbit, Run*), or mythical (*The Centaur*), proceeds from an individual belief that the act is possible. The chief significance of Updike's fourth novel, *Of the Farm* (1965), is the doubt that ceremony is still possible.

The plot recounts a weekend visit of Joey Robinson, his second wife Peggy, and her son Richard to the Robinson family farm in the Dutch country of eastern Pennsylvania, where Joey's recently widowed mother awaits them. The occasion for the visit is the need to cut the high weeds that have overrun the farm since Joey's father died. The action of the novel is a complex and continuous assault on Joey's loyalties to new wife, old wife, children, mother, self, and regional past. Peggy and his mother wish to define him, if not to possess him, and he will not even define or possess himself.

Joey is another Rabbit Angstrom, with this vital difference: unlike Rabbit, Joey does not want to feel right about what he does; he simply wants not to feel. His essential activity is the evasion of feeling. With this motive, he sees no ethical dimension to ceremonial activity. Tradition is important only for what he can take from it. Joey refuses to admit the corporate responsibility for his family which a ceremonial attitude requires. The refusal kills the ceremonial connection between self and tradition.

Admittedly, Joey's situation is complex. It is the particularly modern situation of one beset by the contradictory claims of love. Joey is a thirty-five-year-old advertising consultant who must reconcile the conflicting forces of death, inheritance, and sonship with those of profession, remarriage, and divided paternity. Which action is free? Unable to decide, Joey takes refuge in his memories — much as Rabbit did. He muses on his childhood, on his winning Peggy, and on his happy days with Charlie, Ann, and Martha, his children by his first wife.

The weekend visit to the family farm would seem to be another ceremonial gesture, like the selling of the car in "Packed Dirt." But the farm is no home; vainly trying to recover a sense of his old home, Joey goes out to cut the weeds. But it just won't work. Home and tradition are not subject to recall by empty rituals. The ceremonial gesture of cutting the weeds is only an evasion of his duty to accept the responsibilities of love.

Joey's is a failure in moral nerve. In recompense he attempts to be precise in everything he says, but that precision is purely cerebral—confined to the nuances of sense impression, voice, and gesture. Such precision becomes a kind of grand imprecision when they substitute intellection for love. With such a character it is difficult to determine the values implied by the author, and this is the principal difficulty with *Of the Farm*.

Consider a passage where Joey tells his mother that he will bring Charlie, Ann, and Martha to see her in the fall. His mother interprets the statement as a disloyal act to Peggy; furthermore, she says that she does not expect to see Joey or Peggy again, either. Mrs. Robinson is posturing, but Joey either does not realize it or he does not care. Now if we assume that both his mother and his children matter to him, then he must care, and he must decide whether love compels him to arrange the visit. At the very least he must interpret his mother's turnabout to himself. Instead he indulges his sensibility and his penchant for precision:

> This window, giving on the most lonely side of the house, where the grass was softest and where Peggy had lain, bore on its sill a toy metropolis of cereal and dogfood and bird-seed boxes, whose city gates were formed by an unused salt-and-pepper set of aqua ceramic I had sent from Cambridge fifteen years ago. It was a window enchanted by the rarity with which I looked from it. Its panes were strewn with drops that as if by amoebic decision would abruptly merge and break and jerkily run downward, and the window screen, like a sampler half-stitched, or a crossword puzzle invisibly solved, was inlaid erratically with minute, translucent tesserae of rain.

Does Joey feel anger at his mother? A desire to reassert that he will bring the children in the fall? Did he make the offer to begin with merely to assuage her grief? We do not know—and neither, I suspect, does John Updike. All Joey feels is "ulterior mercy"—but why? And for whom? And what will he do about it?

The emotional groping and the timid maneuvering of these three characters are believable enough. But Updike undermines his characters here. We cannot believe that they have ever loved each other. All dialogue, all action is defensive. Memory isolates; it does not reinforce experience. Mrs. Robinson will not relinquish her dream of the farm as a family saga; Peggy must defend her life with her first husband, McCabe; Joey must protect himself from an exclusive definition as son, lover, or father until he is able to find the right combination for himself. These characters are afraid of love's responsibilities, of life in the present —yet the epigraph from Sartre insists upon the need to be free *in* the present.

Perhaps the contrast is the point. But whatever it is, Updike seems to have abandoned the ceremonial elements that he used so well in his earlier work. *Of the Farm* seems to be a withdrawal from the reality that *The Centaur* engaged so wholeheartedly. At best we can say that the fourth novel is experimental and exploratory. In a sense it turns *Rabbit, Run* upside down. Rabbit manifests a hunger for appropriate feeling; Joey Robinson evades feeling altogether.

Updike seems to use style then to protect the characters from emotional commitment. He makes them so aware of the process by which they feel that they are afraid to feel at all. They seem too conscious of being characters in a novel—which brings us back to our original problem, John Updike's search for a center.

If *The Centaur* offered him a way to resolve style and feeling, it was not a permanent way. The father who is so important in that book (and in most of Updike's fiction) is altogether missing from *Of the Farm*. The novel gives us a neurotic Peter Caldwell without George Caldwell; without a father his son can find no viable context for living.

Indeed, *Of the Farm* suggests that the resources of familial and cultural past are running out for John Updike; once back in New York, Joey Robinson faces affluence and anonymity. True, the mode of the novel is ironic, and we can at least project the desirable alternative, the kind of ceremonial connection which Updike would like his hero to make. Yet that connection seems to be an impossibility now. In this fourth novel, John Updike questions the very sources of personal renewal.

The ability to question one's assumptions is a sign of artistic and personal maturity, of course—and it may be that *Of the Farm* marks a transitional state in Updike's artistic growth. Like Cheever's narrator at the end of *The Wapshot Scandal*, Joey Robinson is closing a chapter in his life. He stands in a balancing position, between childhood loyalties to a farm that is becoming a commodity ("when you sell my farm, don't sell it cheap. Get a good price") and an uncertain future ("down the road, along the highway, up the Turnpike"). Perhaps Joey's uncertain position is the only one available to show the complex and contradictory claims of love.

For both Cheever and Updike, at any rate, ceremonial style is only a tentative resolution of the problem with which we began. An entirely ordered and ceremonial fiction would be as formal (and as lifeless) as a minuet. Yet their achievement to date rests largely on their artistic projection of the conflict between the past and the present, the traditional and the new, and on its brief resolution in ceremonial moments. For them both, style is a way of experiencing the pressures of modern life. If style cannot resolve those pressures, it can at least present them as they are.

DAVID LODGE

Post-Pill Paradise Lost:
John Updike's Couples

Discussing some books about Utopia recently, I ventured the suggestion that "Eros is traditionally an anti-utopian force, though he is catered for in the specialized utopias of pornography—what Steven Marcus has called 'Pornotopia.'" I used the word "traditionally" because we have seen in modern times the emergence of a school of thought that may properly be termed "utopian," in that it is concerned to construct ideal models of the good life, but which inverts the values we normally associate with Utopia, recommending not the enhanced exercise of rationality but the liberation of instinct, not the perfecting of the mind, but "the resurrection of the body." The latter phrase is adopted by Norman O. Brown as a concluding slogan in *Life against Death* (1959), a representative text of the new utopianism. It is not, of course, wholly new, and may be readily traced back to earlier sources—to Nietzsche, to Lawrence and, preeminently to Freud, on whom *Life against Death* is a commentary.

Brown begins with the paradox propounded by Freud, that civilization or "culture" (which is prized by traditional utopists, and which they wish to perfect) is based on the repression and sublimation of erotic energy. Freud himself was shifty about the proportionate loss and gain of this process, but Brown is quite certain and uncompromising: civilization is self-evidently neurotic, and the only solution is to end the tyranny of the reality-principle, to substitute "conscious play" for alienated labour as the mainspring of society, and to restore to adult sexuality, narrowly fixated on genital and procreative functions, the "polymorphous perverse" of infantile eroticism. This utopian adaptation of Freud both

From *The Novelist at the Crossroads and Other Essays on Fiction and Criticism*. © 1971 by David Lodge. Cornell University Press, 1971.

feeds and is fed by the sexual revolution in contemporary society, and the third
interacting contribution comes from the arts. Thus, in this perspective, pornography is the product of a sexually repressed society and would disappear in the
erotic utopia by a process of assimilation. Not surprisingly, therefore, we are
witnessing today a determined effort by the arts to render pornography redun-
dant by incorporating its characteristic materials into "legitimate" art.

John Updike's *Couples* seems to me likely to be best understood and appre-
ciated against this kind of background. It is concerned with the efforts of a
number of couples in contemporary New England to create a clandestine, erotic
utopia; and it is, notoriously, a serious novel which exploits extensively the
matter and diction traditionally reserved for pornography. As this latter feature
would suggest, the utopian enterprise is treated with a good deal of sympathy;
and the novel is notable for its lyrical celebration of the sensual life, including the
"perverse" forms of lovemaking. But whereas Brown, at the outset of his book,
asks the reader to make a "willing suspension of common sense," Updike is, as a
novelist, basically committed to realism (however much heightened by mytho-
poeic allusion) from which common sense—and the reality principle—cannot
be excluded. Thus in *Couples* the note of celebration is checked by irony, the
utopian enterprise fails on a communal level, and the struggle of life against
death is ambiguously resolved.

Erotic utopianism is, of course, at odds with conventional Christian morality and with the Christian counsels of perfection through asceticism; yet at the
same time it claims to be basically religious in its values, and to have in common
with "true" Christianity a virtuous indifference to worldly and materialistic
standards of achievement and success. It thus draws on the Christian tradition of
a prelapsarian paradise, which in turn has literary associations with the ideal
world of pastoral. This matrix of ideas is kept constantly before us in *Couples*,
sometimes lightly—as when the hero's first mistress stills his fears about conception with the gay greeting, "Welcome to the post-pill paradise"—and sometimes
gravely, as in the epigraph from Tillich:

> There is a tendency in the average citizen, even if he has a high
> standing in his profession, to consider the decisions relating to the
> life of the society to which he belongs as a matter of fate on which
> he has no influence—like the Roman subjects all over the world in
> the period of the Roman empire, a mood favourable for the resur-
> gence of religion but unfavourable for the preservation of a living
> democracy.

The couples of Tarbox, a "pastoral milltown," a "bucolic paradise" as it is variously called, within commuting distance of Boston, reenact or parody the situation of the early Christians. "We're a subversive cell . . ." their "high-priest" and "gamesmaster," Freddy Thorne, the dentist, tells them. "Like in the catacombs. Only they were trying to break out of hedonism. We're trying to break back into it. It's not easy." It's not easy partly because the Christian religion still retains a vestigial hold over them. Of the Applebys and the Smiths, who first develop the protocol of wife-swapping, and earn the corporate title of the "Applesmiths," Janet Appleby develops an "inconvenient sense of evil" which the other three try patiently but unsuccessfully to assuage. The main characters, and most adventurous explorers of the erotic, Piet Hanema and Foxy Whitman, are also the most regular churchgoers of the group. Piet, indeed, is burdened with an inherited Calvinist conscience, much obsessed with death and damnation. This makes him the fitting culture-hero—and as it turns out, scapegoat—of the new cult; for in him the struggle of id against ego and superego is most intense and dramatic.

The sex-and-religion equation—sex as religion, sex versus religion, sex replacing religion—is insisted upon even in the topography of Tarbox, with its streets called Charity and Divinity leading to the landmark of the Congregational Church with its "pricking steeple and flashing cock." At the end of the story this church is destroyed by lightning in a furious thunderstorm that has overtones of Old Testament visitations upon sinners; but the damage reveals that the church has long been structurally unsound—in other words, the religious spirit has already passed into the intimate circle of the couples. "He thinks we're a circle," Piet's wife Angela says of Freddy Thorne, "A magic circle of heads to keep the night out . . . He thinks we've made a church of each other." The American couples, however, though they copy the early Christians' withdrawal from the public world in which secular history is made, lack their innocence and confidence. They are apt to feel that they are rejected rather than rejecting. "God doesn't love us any more," Piet asserts. Their magic circle is, in this light, not the seed of a brave new world but a temporary resource "in one of those dark ages that visit mankind between millennia, between the death and rebirth of the gods, when there is nothing to steer by but sex and stoicism and the stars."

This ambivalence is maintained by the two alternative notes that sound throughout the narrative: romantic-lyrical celebration, and realistic irony. The honorific description of the couples' attempt to "improvise . . . a free way of life" in which "duty and work yielded as ideals to truth and fun. Virtue was no longer sought in temple or market place but in the home—one's own home and the home of one's friends," is balanced by the more reductive comment, "The men had stopped having careers and the women had stopped having children.

Liquor and love were left." Adultery opens the way to erotic delight which is far
from being selfish or brutalizing, for in changing partners the aging couples
achieve an enhanced awareness of their own and other's beauty:

> Harold believed that beauty was what happened between people,
> was in a sense the trace of what had happened, so he in truth found
> her, though minutely creased and puckered and sagging, more beauti-
> ful than the unused girl whose ruins she thought of herself as in-
> habiting. Such generosity of perception returned upon himself; as he
> lay with Janet, lost in praise, Harold felt as if a glowing tumour of
> eternal life were consuming the cells of his mortality.

But adultery also imposes its own demeaning code of intrigue and stylized
deception:

> "Are you sleeping with Janet?"
> "Why? Are you sleeping with Frank?"
> "Of course not."
> "In that case, I'm not sleeping with Janet."

The paradoxes and tensions of the theme are most dramatically enacted by Piet
Hanema (partner in a Tarbox building firm) and Foxy Whitman (wife of a
frigid biochemist who is still competing in the "real" world, and hence hostile to
the world of the couples). They dare, erotically, more than any of the other
couples. Their affair is both the most romantically intense and the most sensual
(their oral-genital lovemaking given an extra quality of polymorphous perversity
by the circumstance that Foxy is heavily pregnant by her husband); but they also
suffer most, both comically and tragically. Mastered by an overwhelming desire
to suck the milk-filled breasts of his mistress at a party, Piet locks himself in the
bathroom with her, and escapes discovery by his wife only by leaping from the
window, straight into the arms of another, sardonically teasing couple—hurting
his leg into the bargain. Later in the story a stiffer and more traditional price is
paid for sexual indulgence: Foxy, untypically in the post-pill paradise, fails to
take contraceptive precautions in her first postnatal encounter with Piet, and
becomes pregnant by him. An abortion, with all its attendant anxiety, misery
and guilt, is arranged, but fails to conceal the affair. Piet and Foxy are banished
by their respective spouses, and cold-shouldered by the other couples, whose
disregard for convention does not extend thus far, and who cannot forgive them
for making the clandestine cult scandalously public. They go through a bad
time; but when the wrath of God that Piet has always feared finally strikes, it
does so harmlessly, merely symbolically, on the empty church. After their temporary purgatory of exile and separation, Piet and Foxy are allowed to marry,

and settle happily enough in another town where, "gradually, among people like themselves, they have been accepted, as another couple."

Updike is, of course, neither the first nor the last American writer to take as his subject an attempt (usually unsuccessful) to found a new kind of human community, one based on values that run counter to those prevailing in society at large. The place of *Couples* in this tradition is not immediately apparent only because the utopian experiment it describes is interpersonal rather than social or economic, and thus, on the outside, scarcely distinguishable from the way of life it is rejecting. Utopian communities usually signal their intentions more openly: thus, the middle-aged radicals in Mary McCarthy's *A Source of Embarrassment* set off in covered station wagons to found an agricultural cooperative, and the hippies in the movie *Alice's Restaurant* set up their commune in a deconsecrated church. The tradition can be traced right back to *The Blithedale Romance* (1852), and it is interesting to place *Couples* beside that earlier account of "an exploded scheme for beginning the life of Paradise anew" in New England.

Like Updike's couples, Hawthorne's characters have opted out of the competitive, acquisitive rat race. The narrator, Coverdale, explains: "We had left the rusty iron framework of society behind us; we had broken through many hindrances that are powerful enough to keep most people on the weary treadmill of the established system." In both novels the utopian experiment founders, eventually, on the reef of sex and sexual intrigue. In *The Blithedale Romance* Coverdale is in love with Priscilla who is in love with Hollingsworth who is in love with Zenobia who is secretly and unhappily married(?) to Westervelt who has a mesmeric hold on Priscilla. Coverdale might almost be describing Tarbox when he says:

> the footing on which we all associated at Blithedale was widely different from that of conventional society. While inclining us to the soft affections of the golden age, it seemed to authorise any individual, of either sex, to fall in love with any other, regardless of what would elsewhere be judged suitable and prudent.
>
> (chap. 9)

There are differences, obviously enough. Blithedale is, officially, dedicated to work rather than play, and its play never becomes overtly erotic. Nevertheless, *The Blithedale Romance* contains some of Hawthorne's sexiest writing. Coverdale, for instance, is naughtily given to imagining Zenobia in the nude:

> Assuredly, Zenobia could not have intended it—the fault must have been entirely in my imagination. But these last words, together with something in her manner, irresistibly brought up a picture of that

fine, perfectly developed figure, in Eve's earliest garment. Her free,
careless, generous modes of expression often had this effect of creating images which though pure, are hardly felt to be quite decorous
when born of a thought that passes between man and woman. . . .
One felt an influence breathing out of her such as we might suppose
to come from Eve, when she was just made, and her creator brought
her to Adam, saying, "Behold! here is a woman!" Not that I would
convey the idea of especial gentleness, grace, modesty and shyness,
but of a certain warmth and rich characteristic, which seems, for the
most part, to have been refined away out of the feminine system.

(chap. 3)

Coverdale thinks Zenobia should pose for sculptors, "because the cold decorum
of the marble would consist with the utmost scantiness of drapery, so that the
eye might chastely be gladdened with her material perfection in its entireness."
Looking at "the flesh-warmth over her round arms, and what was visible of her
full bust" he sometimes has to close his eyes, "as if it were not quite the privilege
of modesty to gaze at her." And he is sure that she is sexually experienced:
"Zenobia is a wife; Zenobia has lived and loved! There is no folded petal, no
latent dew-drop, in this perfectly developed rose!" (chap. 6).

There is no such carnal element in Coverdale's "love" for Priscilla—who is,
indeed, precisely the kind of desexualized Victorian maiden with whom Zenobia
is contrasted in the first of these quotations. He apologizes for his suspicions
about Zenobia: "I acknowledged it as a masculine grossness—a sin of wicked
interpretation, of which man is often guilty towards the other sex—thus to
mistake the sweet, liberal, but womanly frankness of a noble and generous disposition." But his suspicions prove well-founded, and Hawthorne evidently
shared his narrator's mixture of guilty excitement and genteel *pudeur* when
contemplating a fully sexual woman, since he is at pains to present Zenobia as a
kind of witch, and sends her eventually to a sudden and sadistically relished
death by drowning.

Updike, in contrast, is much more "emancipated," much more tolerant and
sympathetic towards the erotic, and lets his lawless lovers off lightly in the end.
But there is something of the witch about Foxy, something sinister and depraved,
Lamia-like, about the magnetism she holds for Piet, who is himself quite as
much haunted by the God of Calvin as any Hawthorne hero. Indeed, the more
one dwells on the comparison, the more plausible it becomes to see Hawthorne
as Updike's literary ancestor among the classic American novelists. Both writers
like to temper romance with realism, lyricism with irony; both tend to rely
on ambivalent symbolism at crucial points in their narratives; both are highly

literary, highly self-conscious stylists, fussing over every word to a degree that can be self-defeating; and both seem at their best in the short story, overextended in the long narrative.

Updike's literary gifts, especially his remarkably precise, sensuous notation of the physical texture of ordinary experience, are well suited to the evocation of a suburban pastoral paradise with a snake in the grass. The descriptions of Tarbox, its couples and their way of life—the neglected beauty of the landscape, the comfortable elegance of the expensively remodelled homes, the casual entertaining, the ball games and parlour games, the plentiful food and drink, the intimate uninhibited conversations, as the children watch the blue flickerings of the TV bring meaningless messages of remote disasters and upheavals in the outer, public world (only the assassination of J. F. Kennedy, whose combination of personal stylishness and political weakness makes devious claims on their allegiance, disturbs the couples' calm assumption that "news happened to other people")—all this is exquisitely rendered, so that we feel the charm, the allure of this way of life, and also its weakness, its fragility. The most eloquent passages in the novel are elegiac—for example:

> Foxy said, "We must get back," truly sad. She was to experience this sadness many times, this chronic sadness of late Sunday afternoon, when the couples had exhausted their game, basketball or beachgoing or tennis or touch football, and saw an evening weighing upon them, an evening without a game, an evening spent among flickering lamps and cranky children and leftover food and the nagging half-read newspaper with its weary portents and atrocities, an evening when marriages closed in upon themselves like flowers from which the sun is withdrawn, an evening giving like a smeared window on Monday and the long week when they must perform again their impersonations of working men, of stockbrokers and dentists and engineers, of mothers and housekeepers, of adults who are not the world's guests but its hosts.

This passage illustrates very well how Updike has taken a large abstract theme about contemporary culture and embodied it in a densely textured novel about a particular social milieu. On this level, and as long as he keeps our interest distributed fairly evenly over a considerable number of characters, *Couples* seemed to me remarkably successful. But in the latter half of the book the whole weight of the theme and structure is shifted on to the shoulders of Piet and Foxy, and they are not sufficiently realized to sustain it. Foxy is acceptable as a beautiful witch, but as a Héloïse to Piet's Abélard, analysing her feelings in long, fey epistles, she becomes something of a bore. Piet is more solidly drawn, but his passiveness in the crisis of his marriage induces tedium; and Updike's incorrigible greed for stylistic effect makes nonsense of his attempt to portray his hero as a kind of primitive, a rough diamond who doesn't really belong among the college educated couples. Walking on the shore, for instance, Piet notices

> Wood flecks smoothed like creek pebbles, iron spikes mummified in the orange froth of oxidization, powerfully sunk horseshoe prints, the four-lined traces of racing dog paws, the shallow impress of human couples that had vanished (the female foot bare, with toe and a tender isthmus linking heel and forepad; the male mechanically shod in the waffle intaglio of sneaker soles and apparently dragging a stick), the wandering mollusk trails dim as the contours of a photograph over-developed in the pan of the tide [etc., etc.].

This is a poet's, not a builder's sensibility. The rather Shakespearean intrigue whereby Freddy Thorne arranges Foxy's abortion in return for a night with Piet's wife, Angela, who obliges without enquiring into the basis of the bargain, seems to violate the probabilities of the rest of the action. This is reminiscent of Hawthorne, and so is the device by which Updike displaces the catastrophe of his story from the human characters to the inanimate church—an effective set piece, but too obviously stage-managed, a purely aesthetic climax where we have been led to expect a moral one.

For all that, *Couples* impressed me as an intelligent and skilfully composed novel on a significant theme, and most of the comment I have heard or read upon it seems to me to have done Updike less than justice.

TONY TANNER

A Compromised Environment

For . . . while each cell is potentially immortal, by volunteering for a specialized function within an organized society of cells, it enters a compromised environment. The strain eventually wears it out and kills it.
—*The Centaur*

John Updike seems on first reading to stand quite apart from his contemporary fellow writers. His work reveals no visible need for continually renewed formal experimentation and he seems serenely immune from the paradoxes of the fiction-maker which beset John Barth. For his subject matter he has taken New England suburbia and, at a time when most American novelists seem to regard middle-class life as a desert of unreality, Updike has maintained, and demonstrated, that middle-class existence is more complex than American literature usually allows. Suburbia is the "compromised environment" in which his characters live and to which, like the majority of the American population, they have committed their lives. Just how people live with and within that compromise, and how they die of it, is Updike's avowed subject; and where many contemporary American novelists tend to see the social environment as a generalized panorama of threatening impositions and falsifying shapes, Updike accepts it as the given world for his characters, the one and only locale in which they will learn what they learn and lose what they lose.

In a short story entitled "The Blessed Man of Boston, My Grandmother's Thimble, and Fanning Island" Updike seems to give a clear indication of the kind of fiction he aims to write. It is a story about the subjects of three unwritten stories. The blessed old man is a figure he recalls having seen just for a moment

From *City of Words: American Fiction 1950–1970.* © 1971 by Tony Tanner. Harper & Row, 1971.

at the end of a baseball game. On the strength of this glimpse, Updike (the narrator-novelist) intended to write an immense book about the old man's life, producing pages of detailed but completely imaginary data about his daily routine and surroundings. The thimble is a real object which the narrator comes across one night. It causes him to embark on a lengthy recollection of his grandmother, her place in the family, and how the generations have changed since her time. He wants to write about her because she existed, because she was unique, and because that uniqueness shines out brightly for him now when "identical faces throng the streets." The third unwritten story was to be about a remote Pacific island and a crew of men who once drifted there and were never able to sail away again. There was no woman with them. They lived in unprocreative indolence and slowly died off. The narrator-writer says that it could have been a happy story if he had managed to tell it. In effect, it would be a dream of permanent hibernation, an irreversible retirement from the compromised environment of society—with all the peace and sterility that such a state would entail. Similarly, it is worth noting that part of the blessedness of the Man of Boston was his imagined bachelorhood. Clearly the idea of opting out of all the complications attendant on reproduction is an attractive dream. But, as clearly, Updike is more the writer of the second story, concerning marriage, children, the relationship between generations, and the difficulties and satisfactions of familial continuity. (See for instance his excellent novella *Of the Farm* [1965].) All three stories were going to be full of details ("Details are the giant's finger"), and this indeed is the technique which Updike applies in his own work. What this short story seems to be implying is that the narrator may well be drawn to dreaming of existences very unlike his own. He can give a detailed account of a completely imaginary life in contemporary society; or a detailed account of some exotic retreat from society altogether; or a detailed account of the kind of experience he and his family have had within American society. Updike's details fall mainly in the third category.

The perspectives of his books are all from within the society he knows, whereas most American writers take up perspectives very much more from without it. One stylistic result of this is that the things of this society seem to be perceived, named and related as they would be by the inhabitants of that society; whereas most contemporary American writers find it necessary to submit society to their own particular distortions or patternings and to formulate a personal style in which they can recreate it in their own terms. If one adds to this the fact that Updike is one of the very few contemporary American writers to acknowledge that he is a believing Christian, one can begin to understand how he has acquired something of a reputation for being almost too impeccably orthodox and perhaps too well adjusted to the suburban world and minds he writes about.

John Barth once described Updike as the Andrew Wyeth of contemporary American writers, adding that he arouses the same admiration and reservations; and one can see the aptness of the comparison. In Updike's books there is that same accumulation and momentary arrest of things, that same effect of lacquered stillness in some of the descriptions, and that heightened sense of topographical detail that one associates with Wyeth. "Overhead, held motionless against the breeze, its feet tucked up like parallel staples, a gull hung outlined by a black that thickened at the wingtips. Each pebble, tuft, heelmark, and erosion gully in the mud by the church porch had been assigned its precise noon shadow." That could be a description of a painting by Wyeth. In both men one finds that same wholesale immersion in the details of a well-known locale which sometimes produces a sense of the wonder and strangeness of a world of objects distributed in space, and at other times gives the impression of a brilliantly tessellated surface over a void. And both men have aroused suspicions of meretriciousness through the amazing facility of their technique.

And yet Updike's work contains more than the recognition that most Americans live and die in suburbia and experience all their joys and fears within its ailing routines and often numbing geometries. Norman Mailer, who predictably dislikes Updike's prose and his "pietisms," nevertheless sees there is something else in his work. "The pity is that Updike has instincts for finding the heart of the conventional novel, that still-open no man's land between the surface and the deep, the soft machinery of the world and the subterranean rigors of the dream." The vocabulary is Mailer's, and it is his own ambition to work that no-man's-land he describes, but he is right in saying that behind the attention lavished on the "soft machinery of the world" there is another dimension of feeling in Updike's work. He might seem too much at home in suburbia but, after a little reading, his books start to reveal preoccupations and patterns of feeling and apprehension very similar to some of those we have found in his more obviously worried and experimental contemporaries. Updike's prose does give the impression of being a somewhat rococo version of fairly conventional naturalism, but at its best it is edged with dread. This dread stems from related sources: a terror at the sense of the infinite spaces in which the world tumbles, and the horror which attaches to what he thinks of the Darwinian demonstration that "the organic world, for all its seemingly engineered complexity, might be a self-winnowing chaos."

These feelings of cosmic vertigo seem to feed the basic dread in Updike's work—the fear of death, the fact of decay and the inevitable collapse into nothingness. This produces what he once called "a panicked hunger for things" which will stabilize him as it stabilizes his characters. Harry Angstrom in a moment of worry and apprehension reaches out to touch things "to give himself the small answer of a texture" (*Rabbit, Run*), which is exactly what Updike's prose does as it moves with sometimes hallucinatory alertness among the proliferating objects and surfaces of the suburban landscape. But there are possibilities of dread there as well, for things decay as well as people. What gives a disturbed urgency, characteristic of his best writing, to Updike's apparently suave dealings with things, is a continuous awareness, like an undertow, "that things do, if not die, certainly change, wiggle, slide, retreat, and . . . shuffle out of all identity." Harry Angstrom has a nightmare about a crying girl "and to his horror her face begins to slide, the skin to slip slowly from the bone, but there is no bone, just more melting stuff underneath": it is remarkably similar to the Invisible Man's dream of the girl turning into running jelly and it shows that Updike too shares that nightmare of formlessness, of the progressive fading of all identities, which grips so many other contemporary American writers. And it is not only the loss of human identity that produces the moments of metaphysical dread; there is a more embracing sense of the world slowly submerging into the "melting stuff underneath." The universal fact of continuous erosion falls like a shadow across Updike's mid-century American suburbia. "Waste" is a crucial word and obsession in his work, and his sense of the pathos and horror of a wasting world brings him into unexpected relationship with writers like Pynchon. Updike has also had his vision of an entropic world and in his best work it is what prevents both his prose and his characters from feeling too much at home among the soft machinery of the world.

His first novel was *The Poorhouse Fair* (1959), an original little drama of people moving slowly towards their last repose who still retain enough tenacious will to live to put on their annual poorhouse fair. Updike's own acknowledged preoccupation with the fact of death was surely in part responsible for the rather unexpected phenomenon of a brilliant young *New Yorker* writer choosing to write about an old people's home in his first novel. Instead of yet another subjective monologue about the feelings and worries of youth, Updike imagines the thoughts and actions of a group of people very near the edge of all the mysteries. It may be noted from the start that although Updike's work is, as he admits, deeply rooted in his own familial and territorial experience, he never gives the impression of being imprisoned in the self which is so common in many other American writers. No matter how much refracted autobiography gets into his novels, he does make an unusual bid to explore other minds, and the differing pressures of life on people of different ages. He does this, let it be said, with varying success, but it should be recognized that he has avoided the turmoil experienced in the dwindling tunnel of self by other writers. To those to whom this turmoil is the most real experience they know, this avoidance may well look like an evasion; and to see Updike doing so easily what they feel can scarcely be done at all has led many of his contemporaries to regard his work very equivocally. Yet few, I think, would deny the originality and success of much of his early work.

The Poorhouse Fair starts with one of the old people, Gregg, complaining about the name tags that the new prefect of the poorhouse, Conner, has had put on the chairs. It suggests a routinizing and disciplining of the old people which variously offends their still active sense of themselves as individuals; and the whole book is really a struggle between Conner's humanitarian but abstract notions of patterning, and the old people's vital, if sometimes seemingly perverse, instincts to wander free of them. Conner is a man of the future. He has "lost all sense of omen," and regards existence as something of a vast mess extending backwards through time and across space which is amenable to more or less indefinite clearing up as dictated by the enlightened, scientific human mind. Just noting all the horrible things that can happen to the present human form in its stages of decay makes him assert that " 'Life is a maniac in a closed room,' " and the only heaven he can believe in is a future in which cleanliness and order reign, and suffering has been eradicated. " 'There will be no waste. No pain and above all no *waste*.' " It should be realized that many of these sentiments overlap with ones which Updike himself has avowed—particularly the fear of nature's endless and indifferent wastings—and it is wrong to see Conner as a totally unsympathetic figure. But in him a dislike of mess and dirt has been taken to the point of an antipathy to life itself. At one point the foul-mouthed rebel Gregg introduces a horribly wounded and mutilated cat into the institution. The motive for this is simply "a disturbance of accustomed order." In this cat, Conner sees primarily its disfigurement and probable disease and he orders it to be shot, because "he wanted things *clean*." When he hears the gunshot it pleases him, "anxious to make space for the crystalline erections that in his heart he felt certain would arise, once his old people were gone." It is Conner who accepts the theory of "entropia, the tendency of the universe toward eventual homogeneity" which was discussed in a previous chapter. His shortcoming is that he feels no dread, only distaste.

Conner has his office in a remote cupola which affords him a comprehensive "inclusive" view. The preference for regarding things from a distance is in itself indicative of a disposition to see things in patterns. It is symptomatic of his attitude that when he goes down among the old people setting up their tables in preparation for their annual fair, he notices that the tables are "poorly aligned," and suggests that they be rearranged. Hook, the most authoritative of the senior inmates, a man of faith representing an older America, says to Conner, " 'I have sometimes thought, had you and your kind arranged the stars, you would have set them geometrically, or had them spell a thought-provoking sentence.' " Hook

can still look at nature sensing that there are mysteries beyond the legible regularities of man-made patterns and propositions. And despite various unforeseen
accidents and upsets, the fair, in all its harmless disorder, takes place.

From the elevation of Conner's window "the people in the crowds appear
to bumble like brainless insects, bumping into one another, taking random hur-
ried courses across the grass." The crystalline geometries of Conner's rationalistic
dreams have to concede the day to the apparently brainless randomness of life at
the fair. Updike has said in an interview [in *The Paris Review*, Winter 1968]
that the carnival atmosphere of the last pages of the book, with its merging
fragments of multiple conversations, reminds him a little of the opera ending of
Barth's *The Floating Opera*—"a brainless celebration of the fact of existence"—
and we may recall that this carnival atmosphere appears in the work of another
novelist who has been deeply affected by visions of entropy, William Burroughs.
In their different ways these writers share what seems to be a common feeling
that the carnival (or funhouse or circus) can serve to stand for some of those
instincts in life which resist rigid patternings—of authority, of thought, of some
hostile force—with a randomness and sportiveness of motion (though in Burroughs the image is ambiguous as I have tried to show [elsewhere]). The fair—
any fair—is counter-entropic and counter-crystalline.

At the same time one notes that in what Updike himself has called a latter-
day version of the stoning of St Stephen, Conner is the man who is stoned by the
rebellious inmates, albeit their throwings are fairly inept and the wound is more
psychological than physical. Just how far Updike intends to extend the analogy
between Conner and the first Christian martyr is not clear. From one point of
view it might seem to suggest a vindication of Conner and a vilification of the
old people which Updike can hardly intend. It is perhaps because Stephen was
also, in a way, the first Christian administrator that Updike invoked the comparison, suggesting at the very least that it has always been a thankless task to
run the necessary institutions of society, particularly the ostensibly benevolent
ones. But one of the inmates does seem to speak out for virtues which Conner
neglects, and that is Hook. The difference between Conner's and Hook's visions
of life is made almost schematically plain (compare the opposition between
McMurphy and Big Nurse in Ken Kesey's *One Flew over the Cuckoo's Nest*).
Hook speaks out for the better carpentry of fifty years ago, the more dedicated
craftsmanship and more authentic building materials of the past. Christ was a
carpenter and the profession has symbolic meaning for Hook. But rather than
any God-built universe, Conner believes in the laborious and wasteful trials and
errors of evolution. Again Hook speaks out for the value of the suffering which
Conner would eradicate: " 'Far from opposing the existence of virtue, suffering
provides the opportunity for its exercise.' " For Hook, " 'There is no goodness,

without belief. There is nothing but busy-ness.' " In his eyes Conner can never be more than a busy man, one whom Hook wants somehow to help and advise. It is Hook's thoughts which conclude the book. It is as though he wants to hand something on to the younger generation of thinkers before going to his final rest. Until then he and Conner cohabit in one world.

The novel then brings together many tensions and themes in a single action, a single day—faith and science, the American past and the world of the future, untidy life and orderly planning, the mangy cat and the crystalline dream. Aspects of all these oppositions are clarified and momentarily vivified in this seemingly simple and economical description of the day of the poorhouse fair, and the voices and dispositions of many generations are brought together as parts of a comprehensive statement, fragments of one containing scene. The simultaneous presence of two apparently opposed human groupings—the institution and the fair—conveys an appropriate, and entirely unforced, sense of the realities and ramifications of a compromised environment.

How an individual cell can rebel against the compromised environment of an organized society is the subject of *Rabbit, Run* (1960). Harry Angstrom, who as a youth had experienced the joy of unhindered graceful movement in the special space of the basketball court, finds the world thickening around him as marriage and children and the suburban routines bring a weight of responsibility to bear on him. One of his last realizations, just before the book ends, is a succinct formulation of a discovery made by endless American characters before him. "Funny, how what makes you move is so simple and the field you must move in is so crowded." How crowded this particular field is, and how Harry Angstrom attempts to find some personally satisfying mode of motion within it or out of it, is the subject of the novel. I cannot imagine that the "endless circumstantiality" of this particular kind of suburban world has anywhere been rendered with more "density of specification" than in this book. As the prose meticulously itemizes the objects among which Harry moves, so we can feel the accumulating weight of them pressing on his eyes and nerves and thoughts to the point of claustrophobia. Things are observed in minute detail—brands, prices, foods, cars, household appliances and furniture, all are described and identified by name. From the toys littered on the carpet to the gas tanks glimmering in the smoke and the great stretch of brick which is the town seen from above, Updike fills in the whole panorama of near and far so that we seem to experience to the full the total field which is congesting Harry's vision.

The narrative itself is fairly simple. Harry leaves his dull wife and takes up with a tough prostitute; he returns to his wife when she is having their baby, leaves her again as a result of which she gets drunk and accidentally drowns the baby; he returns only to flee once more from the funeral, and on discovering that his mistress is now pregnant he once more starts to run. In their oscillation Harry's movements rehearse that pattern of attempted disentanglement from, and attempted reintegration into, society which has been so marked in the novels we have considered. More than many novelists Updike does considerable justice to all the other people who are adversely affected by Harry's discontinuous manoeuvrings—the women who suffer, the parents who grieve. He manages to show with a fair degree of impartiality and insight the damage done to society when the insurrectionary self refuses the bondage of its undertaken and imposed responsibilities. At the same time he does communicate the unfocused urgency and incipient panic felt by Harry as he senses that something precious and irreplaceable is being drained out of him while the environment moves to entomb him. Updike produces an extensive vocabulary of constriction to this end. From the beginning when he stops to watch some kids playing basketball and realizes his own displacement, Harry feels "crowded." It is a constantly reiterated word and it is echoed by words and phrases describing how Harry feels cramped, closed in, weighed down by liabilities, imprisoned in packed rooms, his energy fading in the constant negotiation of clutter. In walking out on it all Harry thinks he has found a "freedom into which the clutter of the world has been vaporized by the simple trigger of his decision." But it is of course part of the realism of the book that while leaving seems easy, to discover destination is difficult; and decisions which start in simplicity can end in a renewed thickening of the encircling clutter and confusion.

The problem is acted out in all its stultifying circularity when Harry takes a premonitory drive. On impulse one evening he decides to transform a simple errand within the suburban routine (fetching the car from mother's house) into a reckless flight from it. At first it is as though the road is drawing him away, hinting at escape to a sunny mythical south; but he cannot find the right roads or work out a route, and he has trouble maintaining direction. At one point for instance, he finds "he is going east, the worst direction, into unhealth, soot, and stink, a smothering hole where you can't move without killing somebody." In a sense that is the road he is inevitably on, a graphic version of the road to death, and all his attempts to find a way south are small gestures symptomatic of a larger and more desperate effort of avoidance. But he finds that all roads seem to be "part of the same trap." Just as the clutter of the house he has left "clings to his back like a tightening net" so the roads promising release become a net, a trap (both words are often repeated). Since he does not really know where he is heading for he does not know how to get there, and the problem of mapless movement is experienced in all its frustration.

Like many American figures before him Harry starts to get the feeling that no matter how he moves he cannot get free of some kind of system. "The further he drives the more he feels some great confused system, Baltimore now instead of Philadelphia, reaching for him." Looking for some road on which "he can shake all thoughts of the mess behind him" Harry feels the net thickening and is finally brought to a halt, tangled up in a mess of unknown roads. When he tries to find himself on the map, he finds only a picture of the net in which he is lost. "There are so many red lines and blue lines, long names, little towns, squares and circles and stars . . . The names melt away and he sees the map whole, a net, all those red lines and blue lines and stars, a net he is somewhere caught in." The stress on the geometrical shapes is worth noting, for when Harry tears up the map he is giving vent to that revulsion against the prospect of fixed and defining forms, that antipathy to crystallization, which is such a constant reaction among American heroes. Ambushed by geometry, he finds that there is nowhere to go. At this point, and more so later on, Harry comes close to that despair of necessity which is as constant in American literature as the despair of possibility, and, of course, intimately related to it.

After enjoying the space of the basketball court, Harry experiences the social field outside him only as an arena of hostile manipulation—a Burroughs world if without any of the Burroughs imagery. And he feels that there is something precious and unnameable, which is the very essence of the self, that has to be guarded against external manipulation, "He's safe inside his own skin, he doesn't want to come out." We have encountered the retracted and protected self before, and Harry's claim that, " 'All I know is what's inside *me*. That's all I have,' " is a familiar one. But his moments of confidence when he feels free of all external pressure—"Funny, the world just can't touch you"—are short-lived; and his often repeated action of suddenly running is a measure of his growing panic that the world cannot *not* touch you, that all fields (in any world knowable to Harry) are crowded fields. What keeps him away from home the night his wife Janice drowns the baby is not really the search for his mistress: it is the idea that somewhere "he'd find an opening."

But there are no "openings" in this sense, no hidden apertures in the soft machinery of the world which will afford the individual sudden release into pure uncluttered freedom. Harry's realization as a child "that this—these trees, this pavement—was life, the real and only thing" is a moment of enduring truth. Indeed it is one of the truths conveyed by the texture of the book; it can make it suddenly very oppressive so that we share in Harry's panic. The possibility of escaping into spacious edifices erected by the imagination is not here envisaged, and the only moments of temporary illusory escape are provided by authentic sexual experiences. These may, indeed, provide an opening, and on his first night with the prostitute Ruth, Harry feels "He is out of all dimension." Or, as we may perhaps put it, out of all maps and nets, beyond the geometries of time

and space and a thing-packed world. Since such moments cannot be extended
into a programme for everyday living, Harry's movements can have no constructive goal, no destination beyond that of renewed sexual passion. Harry has in-
choate religious feelings which lead him to announce vaguely that behind all the
visible scenery " 'there's something that wants me to find it,' " but there is some
justice in Eccles's reply that " 'all vagrants think they're on a quest. At least
at first.' " It is the old problem for the American hero of whether he can transform "from" into "towards": like many good men before him Harry cannot get
beyond enacting a mode of motion—running, as Augie March and so many
others run.

As Harry comes to realize that he has lost that irrecapturable vitality of
youth, that "it" which he feels alone makes life worth living, he approaches a
mood of resignation. "The best he can do is submit to the system . . . The
fullness ends when we give Nature her ransom, when we make children for her.
Then she is through with us, and we become, first inside, and then outside,
junk." Reminders of decay and decline are constantly turning up in the landscapes Harry moves in—a junk heap, a treeless waste, a derelict house, a roof
covered in litter, a heap of dead stalks; and it is quite clear that Harry experiences
the dread of suddenly realizing he is in an entropic world which comes to so
many of Updike's figures. His particular dismay is to realize how the entropic
process also affects him, turning him into an object of junk where once vitality
flowered. It is part of his dislike of waste and litter that makes Harry by instinct
a tidy man who likes cleanliness, and even at times makes him want to accept
the system and be a model maintainer of its order. But we encounter once again
the paradox that both the regularities and routines of a rigidly ordered world
(geometry) and the waste and litter which accumulate along and across its lines
(shapelessness) are productive of death.

At the close of the book Harry finds himself confronted by a "dense pack
of impossible alternatives." Standing in the streets he imagines a road leading
back to his responsibilities and commitments, back into the heart of the city; and
"the other way . . . to where the city ends." Then: "He tries to picture how it
will end, with an empty baseball field, a dark factory, and then over a brook into
a dirt road, he doesn't know. He pictures a huge vacant field of cinders and his
heart goes hollow." The field of cinders (almost a Pynchon touch) or the suburban net, it is death either way, and it is death that Harry is really in flight
from—unwilling to confront or accept the ancient truth that in the matter of
man's relation to death "away from" and "toward" are the same thing. He looks
around for guide lights away from the darkness. The delicatessen bulb is shining,
but shopping means responsibilities; the church window is dark. On impulse
Harry turns from both buildings and just follows the street lights—the illusion
of an illumined path. " 'I'm on the way,' " is his last communication to Eccles,

after he has run from the funeral into the woods, and his inability to announce the terminal point of his movement is the most eloquent part of the message.

There is another aspect to his running as well. Trying to work out and balance all the worries and counterclaims on him inside society induces unusual feelings of heaviness of self; he feels clots of concern, clots of sin, or simply clogged with himself. It is only by running, that is by refusing any location and denying any stasis, that he can gain a sense of inner freedom and the weightlessness of the world. "Goodness lies inside, there is nothing outside, those things he was trying to balance have no weight. He feels his inside as very real suddenly, a pure blank space in the middle of a dense net." He remembers the relief on the basketball court when no one could touch you because you had passed the ball and "in effect there was nobody there." He is experiencing the emancipation of invisibility. These are his thoughts while running, feelings engendered by the act of running; that paradoxical American dream of being a weightless self, of combining the relish of identity with the purity of unassailable space is momentarily realized. It is almost a flight away from matter—matter being the ultimate trap.

There is a religious aspect to this, and phrases like "the ideal sub-soil to reality" and Harry's questions about " 'the thing behind everything' " testify to the flickering transcendentalism in Updike's own thinking, as well as Harry's need to believe in something more than the crowded field. But the religious dimension is very tenuous in this book and is in turn part of a much deeper ambiguity in Harry's reaction to the materiality of the world. From one point of view he clings to it, almost like a Hemingway character keeping the void at bay. Sometimes the "solidity" of things is welcome, sometimes nauseating. It is part of the painful paradox of this sort of experience that Harry can feel as though he has fallen out of the given world at the same time as he realizes he cannot escape from it; at once alienated and trapped. For all his feelings that the world cannot touch him, it is "a paralyzing sense of reality" which besets him and which starts him running once again at the end of the book. The end is indeed inconclusive, and as far as Mailer is concerned "Updike does not know how to finish." It seems that he blames the author for Harry's own cowardly indecision. But this is an indecisiveness and evasiveness which has a long history in American literature, and Harry Angstrom running is simply one of many modern Huck Finns wanting to quit society and avoid growing up but with no "territory" to light out to. Perhaps Updike is not sufficiently ruthless in tracing out the inexorable end of Harry Angstrom. But he has made the compromised environment real enough to us for us to realize that Harry Angstrom, whatever his decisions or adopted direction, can only run deeper into the trap, closer to the vacant field of cinders.

A great garbage dump stands in the background of Updike's next novel,

The Centaur (1963). The book concentrates on three days in the life of George Caldwell, an ageing schoolteacher who is having to come to terms with his own decline and imminent death. " 'I'm a walking junk heap,' " he says. As a teacher of evolution, Caldwell can think back to the time "when consciousness was mere pollen drifting in darkness" and on to his own annihilation: zero to zero. At one point he questions a pupil on the subject of "erosional agents" and, despite his blundering affection for people and capacity for love, his mind is more preoccupied with nature's wasting than with nature's bounty. " 'I hate Nature. It reminds me of death. All Nature means to me is garbage and confusion,' " he cries out, late in the book, and everywhere he looks the lesson is the same: all things, cars and people alike, revert, fold, fall apart. "Things never fail to fail." Reminders of waste and death and "the many visages which this central thing wears" are subtly omnipresent in the texture of the suburban world.

The basic subject of the book is the behaviour and reactions of a man finally accepting, absorbing, the fact of his own death, and the effect that sombre realization has on him.

> Since, five days ago, Caldwell grasped the possibility that he might die . . . a curiously variable gravity has entered the fabric of things, that now makes all surfaces leadenly thick with heedless permanence and the next instant makes them dance with inconsequence, giddy as scarves. Nevertheless, among disintegrating surfaces he tries to hold his steadfast course.

This description of his shifting perceptual relationship with the things around him is also a good description of Updike's prose which can register things as being both meaninglessly obdurate and scatteringly ephemeral. In one scene he describes Peter watching with fascination the effect made by the shadows of snowflakes in a pool of lamplight. Directly under the light the shadows seem simply erratic, but away from the centre the shadows seem to repeat endlessly the same patterns of falling. It is another version of an experience central to his work; a dual sense of both the shifting plasticity and the steady geometries of existence.

Moving towards the periphery of the illuminated area "Peter does seem to arrive at a kind of edge where the speed of the shadows is infinite and a small universe both ends and does not end." This moment of experience seems to offer an analogue for the more metaphysical concept of the situation of man which underlies the book (Karl Barth's statement that man is "the creature on the boundary between heaven and earth" stands on the title-page). All Updike's books in one way or another are about moving towards that boundary marked by death, that "kind of edge" at which the small universe of a single man, say that of a schoolteacher in an American suburb, ends and—if religious hopes are answered—does not end. Even without any religious certainty it is clear that we live in a world which is always and never ending, full of things evolving and reverting, growing and wasting in mysterious simultaneity, and it is that world which Updike tries to make us aware of behind the almost trivial familiar details of his foreground scenes.

This reaching for a dimension or realm beyond or behind the visible edges of the given, the compromised environment, is manifest in another way by Peter's sense of the existence of two worlds. As an aspiring artist his feelings cannot be very different from Updike's (himself the son of a schoolmaster), and he spends a good deal of time in an imaginary world to compensate for unaesthetic impositions of the actual. Having spent an evening watching slides illustrating cattle diseases, he returns home to take solace from his book of Vermeer reproductions. Again when his father picks up a hitchhiker in filthy disarray, Peter is horrified at this affront to his artistic aspirations. "That my existence at one extremity should be tangent to Vermeer and at the other to the hitchhiker seemed an unendurable strain." This is another version of the mangy cat and the crystal dream cohabiting in the same world. More pleasantly, when he finds he can buy coughdrops made in Alton when he visits the dream city of New York, the unanticipated fusion delights him: "The two cities of my life, the imaginary and the actual were superimposed; I had never dreamed that Alton could touch New York. I put a coughdrop in my mouth to complete this delicious confusion and concentric penetration."

This is a fair hint at the concentric penetrations of the worlds of Greek myth and contemporary suburbia which Updike is attempting in the novel itself. Peter as narrator says, "I was haunted at that age by the suspicion that a wholly different world, gaudy and momentous, was enacting its myths just around the corners of my eyes," and Updike as writer has tried to do justice to this feeling by, at times, keeping two narrative strings vibrating (as a violinist can hold two notes), and at other times making the legendary and the contemporary echo each other, or, as at the beginning and end, merge into each other. The Chiron myth is appropriate to his purposes, not only because of the figure of noble Chiron, wounded and finally giving up his immortality to seek the repose of death; but because the Centaur, crossing the usual classifications (cf. *Giles Goat-Boy*) by being part animal and part man, occupies "a dangerous middle-ground," analogous to that occupied by man in Updike's religious vision. It would be pointless to go through the novel pointing out just where and how Updike has made the mythic and the contemporary echo or interpenetrate. He has in any case added a Mythological Index so that if you cannot always get the clue, you can—as with any published puzzle—look up the answer in the back. What is more interesting to consider is what might be behind this attempt to conflate two worlds, or, as it might more accurately be put, to turn one world into two.

In the [*Paris Review*] interview Updike discussed the different purposes of the mythic parallel in his book: it offers a "counterpoint of ideality" to the everyday drabness, it allows him to make a "number of jokes," and it serves as a serious expression of his feeling "that the people we meet are *guises*, do conceal something mythic, perhaps prototypes or longings in our minds." One remembers Augie March's feeling that we all catch up with legends more or less, and perhaps part of the particular appeal of Joyce for American writers has been his demonstration of how a mythic dimension can be quite consciously subtended from a segment of contemporary experience. It may be one way of checking that vertiginous feeling of placelessness, or nowhereness, which seems particularly prevalent in America. Asked why he had not done more work in this mode, Updike answered, "But I have worked elsewhere in a mythic mode . . . there is the St. Stephen story underlying *The Poorhouse Fair*, and *Peter Rabbit* under *Rabbit, Run*." Two observations seem to me to be relevant here. First of all there is the easy grouping of classical myth, biblical history or legend, and a children's story. To view *Peter Rabbit* as a myth seems to me rather quaint: it is a familiar tale of great simplicity and charm with a tiny (bourgeois) moral and a comfortable ending, but to call it a myth is to propose an unhappy dilution of the meaning of the word. What Peter Rabbit, St Stephen and Chiron do have in common is that they all figure in well-known stories, and although these stories exist in very different worlds (or concern different orders of reality), it seems that Updike identifies them as being equally suitable for his purpose. By placing the lineaments of a familiar story beneath the contemporary incidents he suggests the existence of an extra dimension (back through time, down into common archetypes), which will give depth and resonance to what might seem to be the fleeting contingencies of his suburban settings.

His own statement, during the interview, of the function of these hinted parallels is an attractive one. "I think books should have secrets, like people do. I think they should be there as a bonus for the sensitive reader, or there as a kind of subliminal quavering . . . In any case, I feel the need for this recourse to the springs of narrative, and maybe my little buried allusions are admissions of it." But, and this is the second observation I think one can make, it seems to me that our detection of these allusions has no effect on our reading of the surface story. As was pointed out, the relevance of St Stephen to Conner is rather far to seek, while to push the analogy between Angstrom and the naughty bunny would if anything trivialize the potentially serious problems posed by the book. The more elaborate network of allusions to the Chiron myth, in my experience of reading the book, does nothing to or for the foreground reality which Updike puts before us with his customary meticulous annotations. What I am aware of, in detecting the allusions, is Updike's own delight in his sport and mental agility.

It has been clear from the beginning that it is often in such sport (James's "fun") that we will find the American writer indulging or exploring his capacities (though what sort of book this can lead to when the capacities are formidable and the sport insecurely grounded, I think *Giles Goat-Boy* demonstrates). The more modest bonus which Updike offers his alert readers puts no such strain on the narrative process. But Updike is also what most other American writers are not, a religious writer. Through the dread and need and hopes of his main characters he seems to want to suggest the existence of another world behind this one, another dimension. But while experiencing his incorporation or interweaving of another *narrative* world (mythic or biblical) as a feat of mental ingenuity, even of fiction-making sport (as in Nabokov whom Updike admires), it is hard to place much credence in the references to another, *religious*, world which Updike surely intends seriously. Paradoxically the effect of most of his work is to leave us feeling that there is only one world, and that the wall of detail with which he confronts us looms all too authentically large. Then we as readers can find ourselves claustrophobically ensnared in that ultimate trap of material clutter which he knows and shows so well.

At one of the many parties in *Couples* (1968) the guests are trying to recall the name of Poe's story about the walls squeezing in on a prisoner. They make their usual compulsive banter about the subject and one suggests that it was by " 'I. M. Flat, a survivor in two dimensions.' " But the wall of matter is indeed squeezing in on the contemporary suburb of Tarbox, and the question of loss or retention of dimension is a crucial one. Updike has never before gone to quite such lengths to itemize the dense tissue of appurtenances which makes up the wealthy contemporary American suburb. Piet Hanema is said to believe that there is, "behind the screen of couples and houses and days, a Calvinist God Who lifts us up and casts us down in utter freedom, without recourse to our prayers or consultation with our wills"; it is perhaps symbolic of his retention of older virtues and attitudes that he does at one point pull off some screening doors with his bare hands. But despite the awesome burning of the church which concludes the book (based, I am told, on an actual event) and which might seem to portend the anger or indifference of a God, what we are made to feel behind the screen is not God so much as—once again—death.

Although in this prosperous suburbia people live well muffled lives (" 'We all rather live under wraps,' " says one character), death and decay are subtly pervasive. The details of Kennedy's assassination filter in from the news media though they are barely registered by the couples busy at their games; the death of all those aboard the submarine *Thresher* which sank beyond trace is made a topic of conversation at a dinner party. Piet himself is however very painfully aware of the reality and imminence of death. At unexpected moments he suffers "a dizzying impression of waste" or gets a "sense of unconnection among phenomena and of falling." He has death panics "as he felt time sliding, houses, trees, lifetimes dumped like rubble, chances lost, nebulae turning." Some of the characters seem almost resigned to "the world's downward skid." Freddy Thorne, the rather obviously named dentist who takes a perverse pleasure in drilling away at people's weaknesses, can get sexually excited by thinking of the rotting enamel he deals with every day. " 'Death excites me. Death is being screwed by God. It'll be delicious.' " Angela loves the severe elegance of Freud's *Beyond the Pleasure Principle* because it stresses that we all " 'carry our deaths in us.' " But such adjustments to the fact of irreversible decline are not for Piet and he seeks for some footing among the sliding. In all the general decay and waste two human activities at least seem able, temporarily anyway, to hold out against the inevitable dissolution—building and love.

As we have noted, carpentry has been present from the start in Updike's work, usually representing the values of an older America, and Piet who comes from a family of builders is recognized as a genuinely dedicated carpenter. Grappling with materials—and they are given in great detail—helps Piet to fend off that sense of the void: "he needed to touch a tool. Grab the earth," an echo of that self-stabilizing pragmatism celebrated by Conrad and Hemingway. The sea reminds him of waste, and he prefers well-made frames. "All houses, all things that enclosed, pleased Piet." He draws back from the foaming formlessness of the sea, the shapeless mud of the swamps, and builds inland. He likes the sense of "space secured"; at the same time he recognizes the rape of "sacred ground" involved in putting up a housing estate—"a pampered rectilinear land coaxed from the sea." There is a realization that man can become too caged in his own constructions, and there is some subtle play with the importance of doors, the point of mediation between architecture and space, form and formlessness. One of his affairs gives him the pleasure of "going from indoors to outdoors" and since the women in the book are more usually connected with the flow of the sea and the undefined openness of space, it suggests that the carpenter at times feels the need to escape from his own carpenterings. When his wife calls him a caged animal and Piet retorts, " 'But Angel, who made the cage, huh?' " we surely recall that Piet himself has been shown to be the expert cage-maker (he constructs one for the children's hamster); to some extent the retort recoils on him. For in a larger sense the "cage" or "trap" is simply that compromised environment which he himself works to maintain with his well-made frames.

The other act which counters death is love. To quote from Updike's essays: "A man in love ceases to fear death ... Our fundamental anxiety is that we do not exist—or will cease to exist. Only in being loved do we find external corroboration of the supremely high valuation each ego secretly assigns itself." And the fact that in the act of love it takes two to do just about everything is felt to be the ultimate defence against entropy. "She was double everywhere but in her mouths. All things double. Without duality, entropy. The universe God's mirror." Hence the title *Couples*, and the various references to "The beauty of duality. A universe of twos." It is the desire of these twos to take up mirror positions with one another that makes the world go round. "At the corner two dogs were saying hello. Hello. Olleh." Man is himself a duality—groin and brain—and the large amount of oral sex described in the book is seen as a response to this condition, a ritual meeting of mind and matter. There is clearly a philosophical or biochemical point in Updike's elaborate detailing of the exhaustive sexual permutations acted out by the wealthy inhabitants of Tarbox. In the interview Updike said, "I was struck, talking to a biochemist friend of mine, how he emphasized not only the chemical compositions of enzymes but their structure; it matters, among my humans, not only what they're made of, but exactly how they attach to each other. So much for oral-genital contacts." A concern with structure permeates the book, manifest not only in Piet's carpentry, but Ken Whitman's biochemistry (it is part of Updike's acuteness of observation that he can show how different professions tend to make people think and talk in different ways), and a more general concern about whether matter—from stars to starfish—is chaotic or systematic.

To a man who asks how "a complex structure" can arise spontaneously out of chaos, Ken replies, " 'Matter isn't chaos . . . It has laws, legislated by what can't happen.' " Shortly before he changes his life by marrying Foxy, Piet dreams of ill-fitting frames, structures that will not stay erect. Then he dreams that, "He was standing beneath the stars trying to change their pattern by an effort of his will." In combination these dreams seem to suggest that although the individual may make a mess of the particular patterning of his life in the social and domestic sphere, he is ultimately participating in a vaster, deeper, older pattern from which—along with the starfish and the stars—he is helpless to deviate. Early in the book Foxy thinks of Ken working in his laboratory "down there, where the protons swung from molecule to molecule and elements interlocked in long spiral ladders." Just so, the book seems to imply, the inhabitants of Tarbox interlock in long spiral ladders. Mirrors are much in evidence in the book and one effect they have is to make a single grouping appear like a symmetrical pattern and repetitive process. ("The sliding glass doors . . . doubled their images, so that a symmetrical party seemed in progress.") In all their clumsy, heartless, and often rather cruel and jaded sexual games, the "couples" are to be seen as acting out a pattern which is rooted "down there" in the biochemical sources of life. Without abandoning his felicitous notation of contingent details, which give one that illusion of randomness characteristic of changing social scenes, Updike manages to convey the presence of this underlying pattern.

But just here, I think, a problem obtrudes for the novelist. For to the extent that he suggests the dominance of that pattern he is likely to diminish the sense of the importance of differences between the individual agents who maintain it. From the point of view of the pattern, the dogs at the corner are helping to maintain the universe. Of course, they are; but then from this point of view how is one to differentiate among humans who, in their coupling, are also obeying and preserving the structure of life. From one point of view the novel could be showing how, in the "post-pill paradise," sex, so far from maintaining the universe by leading to procreation, has degenerated into an empty and sterile game. But there are quite a few children scattered around, and when it comes to enjoying fornication divorced from any thoughts of conception Piet is well to the fore. And yet Piet is clearly meant to be in some way the hero of the book, a true lover. Updike surely intends his relationship with Foxy to be a serious love story, but in this world—or the world seen from this point of view—how is sex as love to be differentiated from sex as lust? Nearly all the sexual activity of the book is celebrated lyrically and yet it would seem that a good deal of it is meant morally to be judged adversely, or at least seen as a symptom of some social malaise.

There is a blur in the novel when it comes to this problem, and while the book certainly makes clear the difficulties involved in taking up any definite religious or moral attitudes towards sex in our relativistic age, I think this blur makes the attempt to differentiate Piet as somehow more authentic than the other characters unconvincing. Accused not unjustifiably of weakness by the other couples, there is an attempt to interpret this to mean that his "strengths weren't sufficiently used." To romanticize his adulteries by saying things like "only Piet had brought her word of a world where vegetation was heraldic and every woman was some man's queen," reads like banal literary exoneration. It is not a question of reintroducing a proto-Victorian abruptness and certainty of censure. It is only that one would like to see an important problem brought into focus. What is it that makes one "coupling" better, more humane, more authentic, than another, when from one point of view every coupling is an act of participation in, and preservation of, the universal structure? Perhaps, indeed, we are in need of a whole new vocabulary if we are to discuss the problem adequately, and Updike's novel at least goes some way to exploring the whole problem of "relationships" in contemporary America.

One way in which Updike attempts to give an added dimension to Piet is to suggest his relationship to older prototypical figures. To quote his own words: "Piet is not only Hanema/anima/Life, he is Lot, the man with two virgin daughters, who flees Sodom, and leaves his wife behind." He also says that he was aware of Piet and Foxy as "being somehow Tristram and Iseult" and accepts that Piet may also be Don Juan. Again, I do not see that these references or analogues operate to any great effect in the book; their very multiplicity in itself suggests something a bit too easy. What does serve to mark Piet out is his capacity for dread and his heightened sense of the compromised environment through which he moves. The ending is thus equivocal. He has broken out of his marriage and the Tarbox trap, but only into another marriage and another suburb, "where, gradually, among people like themselves, they have been accepted, as another couple." So the book ends, echoing the first sentence and suggesting the circularity of the whole process.

Updike has stated that he intended the ending to be ambiguous. It is a "happy" ending, since Piet marries Foxy. But by putting his guilt behind him and becoming just another satisfied person Piet "in a sense dies." In elaborating on this Updike made a statement which is relevant for an understanding of all his novels: "a person who has what he wants, a satisfied person, a content person, ceases to be a person . . . I feel that to be a person is to be in a situation of tension, is to be in a dialectical situation. A truly adjusted person is not a person at all." More than any religious implications, it is this feeling which the book communicates most strongly—that to allow the self to be absorbed into the compromised environment is tantamount to losing one's selfhood (a deeply American feeling); at the same time life *in* that environment, with a well-loved wife and a well-built house, is the best antidote to that great cosmic dread and sense of universal waste which besets Updike's characters. Because this fear can be so intense Updike sometimes seems to write in support of the compromised environment, though not without recognizing the ambiguity of what it offers.

It is this qualified, or intermittent, support for the suburban environment which has sometimes provoked the criticism of writers and critics who feel that the writer's repudiation of American society should be more total, or his attack on it go much deeper. Sometimes Updike's prose does take on a slick sheen which to a hostile eye may seem to partake a little of the suspicious polish of the merchandise which clutters the suburban world he writes about. There is no doubting his brilliance and fluency as a prose writer, and there are certain atmospheres, occasions, moods, which he can evoke with incomparable vividness and authority. At the same time there is something decorative and strained about many of his similes—an air of cultivated "fine writing"—which can detract from the impact of his work, giving it at times the timbre of a stylistic exercise. He himself has said that he writes fairly rapidly without much revision and he describes the author's deepest pride, as he has experienced it, "not in his incidental wisdom but in his ability to keep an organized mass of images moving forward, to feel life engendering itself under his hands." I think one can appreciate much of what is good in his writing if one bears in mind this delight in maintained momentum.

As has been clear from the start Updike shares that vision of entropy so common among contemporary American writers. Those of his characters who "run" do so, among other things, from the entropic facts of life. To Freddy Thorne, a "vortex sucking them all down with him," Piet says, " 'I think you're professionally obsessed with decay. Things grow as well as rot.' " This counterbalancing truth is one which it seems unusually hard to hold on to in contemporary American fiction. I would suggest that for Updike writing is a way of holding on to the fact of growth, holding out against entropy. Ken, the biochemist, is trying to approach the mystery of organic life, "chlorophyll's transformation of visible light into chemical energy. But here, at this ultimate chamber, the lone reaction that counterbalances the vast expenditures of respiration, that reverses decomposition and death, Ken felt himself barred." He feels himself facing "an irreversible, constricted future"; the squeezing of the walls of the compromised environment. But Updike in the act of writing is, as it were, overcoming that barrier, and in his own way celebrating or miming that "lone reaction . . . that reverses decomposition and death." He has said that his first thought about art was "that the artist brings something into the world that didn't exist before, and that he does it without destroying something else. A kind of refutation of the conservation of matter. That still seems to me its central magic, its core of joy." Society, as an organized cluster of cells, inevitably shares in the process of entropy; the engendering of a work of art can appear, temporarily, to refute it. In the compromised environment which gradually entraps his characters, it is perhaps Updike himself as the writer who is the most subversive cell. The complaint of some of his critics is that, at times, he is not subversive enough.

JOYCE CAROL OATES

Updike's American Comedies

I must go to Nature disarmed of perspective and stretch myself like a large transparent canvas upon her in the hope that, my submission being perfect, the imprint of a beautiful and useful truth would be taken.

—The Centaur

His genius is best excited by the lyric possibilities of tragic events that, failing to justify themselves as tragedy, turn unaccountably into comedies. Perhaps it is out of a general sense of doom, of American expansion and decay, of American sub-religions that spring up so effortlessly everywhere, that Updike works, or perhaps it is something more personal, which his extraordinary professional art can disguise: the constant transformation of what would be "suffering" into works of art that are direct appeals to the *her* of the above quotation, not for salvation as such, but for the possibly higher experience of being "transparent" —that is, an artist. There has been from the first, in his fiction, an omniscience that works against the serious development of tragic experiences; what might be tragedy can be reexamined, reassessed, and dramatized as finally comic, with overtones of despair. Contending for one's soul with Nature is, of course, the Calvinist God Whose judgments may be harsh but do not justify the term *tragic*.

Like Flannery O'Connor, who also studied art before she concentrated upon prose fiction, Updike pays homage to the visual artist's "submission" to the physical stimuli of his world far more than most writers. He transcribes the world for us, and at the same time transcribes the experience of doing so, from the inside. His world, like O'Connor's, is "incarnational"—vividly, lovingly, at times meanly recorded—perhaps because, in Updike, such a synthesis of fidelity

From *Modern Fiction Studies* 21, no. 3 (Fall 1975). © 1975 by the Purdue Research Foundation, West Lafayette, Indiana.

and inventiveness allows an escape of sorts from the tyrannical, unimaginative cosmology of Calvinism. O'Connor was affirming her faith through allegorical art; Updike usually affirms it in words, but the act of writing itself, the free lovely spontaneous play of the imagination, *is* salvation of a kind. Does the artist require anything further? Updike's prose style resembles Nabokov's, of course, and yet it seems to me that in Updike the activity of art is never for Nabokovian purposes—never to deceive, to conceal, to mock, to reduce Nature to an egoistic and mechanical arrangement of words. On the contrary, Updike seems at times too generous, too revealing. His energies are American in their prolific and reverential honoring of a multitude of objects, as "Nature" is scaled down, compressed, at times hardly more than a series of forms of The Female.

Museums and Women makes the point explicitly that both "museums" and "women" are mysterious structures which, once entered, once explored, somehow lose their mystery; yet they are, to use Peter Caldwell's phrase, "high religious halls" that attract the artist again and again. Flannery O'Connor's interest was in love of a distinctly spiritual nature, but Updike speaks with Alexander Blok, surely, in saying, "We love the flesh: its taste, its tones / Its charnel odor, breathed through Death's jaws" ("The Scythians," epigraph to *Couples*). Because O'Connor's Catholic faith was unshakable, she could invent for her allegorical people ghastly physical-historical fates, assuming that their souls, encompassing but not limited to their egos, were unkillable. Updike's faith is possibly unshakable as well—which, judging from observations scattered throughout his writing, in a way alarms and amuses him—but his sympathies are usually with those who doubt, who have given up hope of salvation as such, wanting instead to be transparent, artists of their own lives. The "beautiful and useful truth" that Peter Caldwell prayed for has little to do with religious convictions, but everything to do with the patient, reverential transcribing of Man comically descended into the flesh: into Nature. Once in the flesh, once individualized, Man can then attempt some form of rebellion against "fate"—enjoying the very absurdity of his position.

The hero of *Couples*, Piet Hanema, is a man of artistic imagination, somehow trapped by his work, his marriage, the unholy and entertaining town of Tarbox, and he is, despite his despair and his promiscuity, a religious man. Foxy tells him that "his callousness, his promiscuity, had this advantage for her; with him she could be as whorish as she wanted, that unlike most men he really didn't judge." Piet answers that it is his Calvinism: "Only God judged." But more than this, Piet believes that God has already judged: it is all over, history, melodrama, comic arrangements and rearrangements of adulterous couples, the Day of Judgment is—as Kafka has said—a perpetual event, the court always in session and the judgments known ahead of time because everything is predestined. Updike understands women well in allowing Foxy to compliment her lover on character traits that, ironically, activate less-than-admirable traits in her, but she speaks more generally for the sly truth that must gradually but inevitably dawn upon the Puritan Calvinist of any intellectual capacity: one can do exactly as one wishes, since salvation or damnation are accomplished facts, impersonal, boring, finally irrelevant. A sense of determinism, whether religious or economic or biological, has personal advantages never dreamt of by those who believe in free will. When Updike explores the non-Protestant possibilities of the imagination, when he sends out his soul, let us say, in the guise of an atheistic Jew, we have the fantastically funny and despairing Bech who, in being elected to a society of arts and letters to which Updike was himself elected in real life, precociously, muses:

> His mother was out there in that audience!
> But she had died four years ago, in a nursing home in Riverdale. As the applause washed in, Bech saw that the old lady . . . was not his mother but somebody else's. . . . The light in his eyes turned to warm water. His applause ebbed away. He sat down. . . . Bech tried to clear his vision by contemplating the backs of the heads. They were blank: blank shabby backs of a cardboard tableau lent substance only by the credulous, by old women and children. His knees trembled, as if after an arduous climb. He had made it, he was here, in Heaven. Now what?
>
> *(Bech)*

Bech is Updike's projection of an Updike unprotected by women, children, God; though attached to his mother, as Updike's characters are often attached to their mothers, he "ascends" to this mock-Heaven only after her death, when it is too late. His adventures must be seen as comic because they are so desperate, so horrible. In this way Updike explores wittily the very real possibilities of a shallow imaginative life "free" of Calvinistic gloom, though it must be said, in my opinion at least, that he does not convince us of Bech's "Jewishness" —Bech is a man without a soul. In the brief reverie "Solitaire," in *Museums and Women*, a husband contemplates leaving his wife for his mistress, but contemplates it only with one part of his mind—the aesthetic; he knows very well that his identity would be lost outside the confining and nourishing circle of wife and children: in fact, he married young, had several children almost at once, in order to assure his being trapped. Bech escaped the trap, but at great cost to his soul.

By isolating those lines from *The Centaur* in which Peter-as-Prometheus speaks so eloquently about submitting himself to Nature, I am deliberately giving more weight to the pagan-classical-artistic-"immoral" side of Updike's imagination than to the Calvinistic, though, in fact, the two are balanced. *The Centaur*, being a relatively early and emotionally autobiographical work, is valuable in its

obvious statement of the dichotomy in the author's imagination between the
"pagan" and the "Christian." Critics may well disagree about the merit of the
uses to which Updike put his childhood interest in "old Greek folk stories told
anew," and surely the example of Joyce's *Ulysses* was always in his mind; but,
unlike Joyce, he did not evoke the classical in order to give structure to quantity
or to comment ironically upon it, but to provide for himself, for Peter, for
George Caldwell, another spiritual dimension in which they might be heroic
without fear of being heretical. Significantly, the "pagan" world is really a
feminine world; Updike alludes to the whimsical and tyrannical figure of Zeus,
but it is Venus Aphrodite who speaks to Chiron at such length in chapter 1 and
even offers to embrace him, though he is part-beast, and Venus Aphrodite in the
form of Vera Hummel, the girls' gym teacher, with whom the young impres-
sionable Peter Caldwell imagines himself "sharing a house" in a concluding
chapter. Venus, not Zeus, presides over the pagan world. Unlike the woman who
awaits Peter and his father back on the farm, in that fertile but uncultivated land
that is more a burden than a place of retreat, Vera Hummel is all warmth,
simplicity, radiance, nourishment. *She*, of course, is promiscuous; Cassie Caldwell is someone's faithful wife, herself trapped, complaining, and bitter and yet,
ultimately, fairly satisfied with her lot. Vera is the promise; Cassie the reality.
Vera forever beckons, but is not known; Cassie is known. Though Peter and his
father return to the farm, and will always return (as the narrator of *Of the Farm*
returns—to betray his wife with his mother!), it is Venus Aphrodite who has the
power of altering lives without exactly touching them. Here is the adolescent
Peter:

> The next two hours were unlike any previous in my life. I share a
> house with a woman, a woman tall in time, so tall I could not
> estimate her height in years, which at the least was twice mine. A
> woman of overarching fame; legends concerning her lovelife circu-
> lated like dirty coins in the student underworld. A woman fully
> grown and extended in terms of property and authority; her presence
> branched into every corner of the house. . . . Intimations of Vera
> Hummel moved toward me from every corner of her house, every
> shadow.

Always outside the masculine consciousness, this archetypal creature when
embodied, however briefly, in flesh, has the power to awaken, however briefly,
the "religious" experience common to the entering of both museums and women;
she is life itself, the very force of life, playful, promiscuous as Nature, ultimately
uncaring as the ancient Magna Mater was so viciously uncaring of the beautiful
adolescent youths she loved and devoured. Contemplating the naked green lady

of the Alton Museum, a fountain-statue, the child Peter is at first troubled by the mechanical logistics of the statue that forbid its ever quenching its thirst; but, artist as he is, manipulator of reality as he will be, he tells himself that at night the statue manages to drink from its own fountain. "The coming of night" released the necessary magic. Because the Venus-figure is experienced as archetypal rather than personal, she is never connected with any specific woman, but may be projected into nearly anyone. She is simple, vital, enchanting, and yet— curiously—she is no threat. Men remain married or, at the most, remarry women with children (like Peggy of *Of the Farm*; like Foxy of *Couples*, one baby alive, one baby aborted, but a mother nevertheless); and as everyone knows Venus is sterile. She has never entered history. Piet Hanema perhaps speaks for Updike in diagnosing his eventual dissatisfaction with one of his mistresses, Georgene, because she made adultery too easy, too delightful, for his "warped nature." And so in *The Centaur*, Venus/Vera attracts her opposite, the Reverend March, he whose faith is so unshakable, intact and infrangible as metal, and "like metal dead." Economically and concisely developed, the Reverend March is a type that appears occasionally in Updike ("The Deacon" is an older, wearier version) and whose function in *The Centaur* is not only angrily to resist the desperate George Caldwell's desire to speak of theological matters at a basketball game, but, more importantly, to be the man whose faith is dead and metallic and yet rather wonderful ("Though he can go and pick it up and test its weight whenever he wishes, it has no arms with which to reach and restrain him. He mocks it.") and whose faith allows him a psychological insight that, in Updike-as-Peter, would be annihilating when he muses upon the fact that a woman's beauty depends only upon the man who perceives her: Her value is not present to herself, but given to her. "Having been forced to perceive this," the Reverend March is therefore "slow to buy."

Because the Feminine Archetype is always projected outward, and the knowledge of this projection ("valuing" or "pricing," in the Reverend March's crude terminology) cannot be accepted except at the risk of emotional impotence, it slips back beneath the level of consciousness and is not accepted at all. It is not seen to be a natural psychological fact in which the perceiver-artist values, creates, and honors everything he sees—not only women—and in which he himself re-creates himself *as* an artist; it is, instead, despairing if and when it is admitted, so grotesque that it had better not be admitted. So, Updike puts into the mouth of Janice Angstrom of *Rabbit Redux* words no woman would say, being in one sense obvious and in another sense completely incorrect: "I'm just a cunt. There are millions of us now." And Bech's horrific vision in "Bech Panics" is the stuff of which religious conversions are made of, so intense and incredulous is his experience of the falsity of an old faith:

He looked around the ring of munching females and saw their bodies
as a Martian or a mollusc might see them, as pulpy stalks of bundled
nerves oddly pinched to a bud of concentration in the head, a hairy
bone knob holding some pounds of jelly in which a trillion circuits,
mostly dead, kept old records, coned motor operations, and generated
an excess of electricity that pressed into the hairless side of the head
and leaked through the orifices, in the form of pained, hopeful noises
and a simian dance of wrinkles. Impossible mirage! A blot on nothingness. And to think that all the efforts of his life—his preening,
his lovemaking, his typing[!]—boiled down to the attempt to dis-
place a few sparks . . . within some random other scoops of jelly.

(Bech)

Bech gives voice to suspicions Updike may play with, but cannot take seriously;
he knows we are not free, and so Bech's lazy "freedom" is mere fiction, the
maniacal cleverness of an intellectual consciousness unhampered by restraint, by
the necessary admission of its subordinate position in the universe. And yet—if
Bech *were* correct—one would be free of the tyrannical father as well, and free
of the need to perform, ceaselessly, the erotic activity that defies him: writing.
For Bech, of course, is a writer who cannot write. Updike may write about him,
but Bech requires a week to compose a three-page introduction to the book.
Free, yes, undamned and unhaunted—but whoever wanted such freedom?

Most of the time, however, the projection is not recognized as such; it is
experienced in a religious manner, the woman is "adored," she is associated with
Nature, as either the Mother herself or a form of the mother, and is in any case
the promise of timelessness within the oppressive context of time. Foxy Whitman
is loved when she is pregnant and because she is pregnant; once delivered of her
child, her "flat" being somehow disappoints and bewilders her lover. Burdened
with the difficult responsibility of making men immortal, the woman-as-adored
either tires of the whole thing (as Joan Maple has grown tired in *Museums and
Women*, itself a curiously tired book) or shares with her adorer a baffled metaphysical rage: *Why* isn't love permanent?

In asking of love that it be permanent, Updike's characters assert their
profoundly Christian and historically oriented religious temperament, for not
many religions have really promised an "immortality" of the ego let alone the
Theistic mechanism to assure this permanence. In Updike, Eros is equated with
Life itself, but it is usually concentrated, and very intensely indeed, in terms of
specific women's bodies; when they go—everything goes! Hence Bech's terror,
his breakdown, hence the fact, "monstrous and lovely," Peter discovers in kissing
his girl, Penny, that at the center of the world is an absence: "Where her legs

meet there is nothing" (*Centaur*). Because he is an adolescent and will be an artist, Peter still values this "nothing" and equates it with "innocence." *He* experiences his own artistry, through this equation, as Chiron/George Caldwell experiences his own divinity by simply accepting, as an ordinary human being, the fact of mortality. *The Centaur* is the most psychologically satisfying of Updike's numerous books—it may or may not be his "best" book—because it has expressed its author's considerable idealism in the guise of adolescent love, for Woman and for Father, an idealism Updike may not trust in adult terms. Or perhaps the world has changed, has become more "adult" and secular and unworthy of redemption—the dismal Tarbox of *Museums and Women* is far less attractive than the same Tarbox of *Couples*, though that was degenerate enough. An earlier novel, *Rabbit, Run*, explored quite remorselessly the consequences of a reduced, secularized, "unimagined" world, Updike's conception of Updike-without-talent, Updike trapped in quantity. But the consciousness of a Rabbit Angstrom is so foreign to Updike's own that it seems at times more a point of view, a voicing of that part of the mind unfertilized by the imagination, than a coherent personality. Rabbit is both a poet and a very stupid young man. A decade later, as Rabbit led back, penned, now finally trapped, he has become an uneasy constellation of opinions, insights, descriptive passages and various lusts, a character at the center of *Rabbit Redux* called "Harry"; he ends his adventure in a motel room with his own wife, Janice, Venus-led-back, he is exhausted, impotent, but agreeable: O.K. The *Yes* of *Ulysses* is the weary O.K. of a man imagined as typically "American."

The world itself has not changed, though history—both personal and collective—has certainly changed. *Couples* dramatizes in infinite, comically attentive detail the melodramatic adventures of "typical" Americans in a "typical" though sophisticated town in New England; love vies with the stock market in reducing everyone to ruins. Much has been said, some of it by the author himself, of the novel's religious and allegorical structure, which is so beautifully folded in with the flow of life, the workings-out of numerous fates, as to be invisible except in concluding scenes: the Congregational Church is struck by "God's own lightning," its weathercock is removed, Piet discovers in the ruins a pamphlet containing an eighteenth-century sermon that speaks of the "indispensable duty" of all nations to know that "the LORD he is God." Piet is not much of a hero, and he does not choose to be heroic. He has, after all, helped arrange for the abortion of a baby both he and his mistress really wanted; but he is one of the few characters in Updike's recent fiction who can somehow synthesize the knowledge of human "valuing" with a religious faith that sustains it while reducing it to scale.

Piet does not require that love be permanent—or even "love." If he is an artist it is at compromises he is best; failing to be an architect, he winds up as a construction inspector for military barracks, failing to keep his wife from divorcing him, he moves on to the next stage, the next compromise. He has not much choice except to compromise his ideal love (Foxy pregnant) with his real love (Foxy the individual). After the desperate violence of his love ebbs he is able to see the woman clearly, not perfect, not even very charming, at times embarrassingly "tough," "whorish" as if performing for him, her waist thickened by childbirth, her luminous being somehow coarsened into the flesh of historical experience. Yet Piet says, without lying, that she is beautiful anyway; he adores her anyway; he marries her and they move to another town where "gradually, among people like themselves, they have been accepted as another couple." The practical wisdom of the novel's concluding sentence may be interpreted as cynicism, or as a necessary and therefore rather comic working-out of events that made their claim for tragic grandeur, but fell short.

In this way Piet accepts his own mortality, a movement into adulthood, middle-age, in which the adolescent yearnings for an inexpressible transcendence in fleshly terms is put aside. In a powerful paragraph at the end of chapter 3 ("Thin Ice"), Piet has already come to terms with his own death by recognizing that "the future is in the sky. . . . Everything already exists" and this knowledge has the effect of undoing some of the magic of Foxy: "Henceforth he would love her less." The "love" he had experienced for Foxy was a form of delirium in which his terror of death was temporarily obliterated in the body of Venus—but only temporarily, for his real allegiance is to doom, to a future already in existence, a God Who manipulates men according to His inscrutable design.

At the same time Piet articulates what is sometimes kept beneath the level of consciousness in Updike: that the infatuation with surfaces, the artist's-eye aspect of his imagination, is somehow less basic to him than a deeper and more impersonal tendency toward unity, toward the general. After Angela has asked Piet to move out of their home he finds himself with a great deal of time, little to do, very much alone; and out of his loneliness the discovery that

> The world was more Platonic than he suspected. He found he missed friends less than friendship; what he felt, remembering Foxy, was a nostalgia for adultery itself—its adventure, the acrobatics its deceptions demand, the tension of its hidden strings, the new landscapes it makes us master.

By a subtle—but not too subtle—shifting from the relatively restricted third person of "he" to the communal "us" Updike invites his readers to admit, in league with his doomed character, that the particular objects of any kind of infatuation, however idealized, are mere stimuli that activate the inborn responses of "love"; Venus Aphrodite is a figure that somehow unites and in that way attempts to explain a bewildering multiplicity of love-urges, but cannot exist "in herself" and cannot be more permanent than the brain-structure in which these love-urges exist. And yet—does it really matter? Lying with Foxy in his squalid rented room, Piet makes comic moaning noises, at first disgusting Foxy and then drawing her into imitating him; and Updike comments, again with an ironically confident nineteenth-century omniscience: *We are all exiles who need to bathe in the irrational.*

In a poem, "South of the Alps," the speaker is being driven to Lake Como by a beautiful Italian woman, is seated in the back of the car, terrified at the woman's careless speed, while "Her chatting lover occupied the death seat." The elements of an essential Updikean romance are present: the woman is seen as an "ikon," her beauty is "deep in hock to time" and reckless with itself, and the men around it, slavish, adoring, hopeless. The poet sees himself as a "cowardly word-hoarder":

> Of course I adored her, though my fate was a midge on her wrist she
> could twitch away; the Old Testament said truly: fear is love and
> love is rigid-making fear.

Unknown in any personal, fleshly sense, unentered, unexplored, Signorina Angeli, an "angel" as finally remote and rejecting as Piet's wife Angela, alarms the poet and has the final line of the poem: "Tell me, why doesn't anything last?" And here it is Venus speaking from the disappointed idealism of the male, promised permanence and yet continually denied it.

"South of the Alps" shows us, in beautifully compressed language, the bewildering locked-in fates of the adorer and the adored: the masculine consciousness that, having failed to integrate the "Feminine" with its own masculinity, seeing it as essentially pagan and heretical, must continually project it outward; the feminine consciousness that, having taken on the masculine, Faustian quest for permanence, must be forever loved, a beloved, an ikon with nostrils "nice as a skull's." Male and female here unite only through a declaration of their common predicament. A writer who shares Updike's extreme interest in the visual world as well as his obsession with language is Joseph Conrad who, significantly, could imagine the ideal, and the real only as hopelessly separate: when the "ideal" is given historical freedom to experience itself in flesh, in action, we have the tragicomedy of *Nostromo*, we have the Feminine Archetype (I use this expression, clumsy as it is, because Conrad nearly uses it himself), Mrs. Gould, at the very center of a storm of mirages, each an "ideal," each a masculine fantasy. But Conrad—ironic and witty as he may be—has not finally Updike's sanity, Updike's redeeming sense of humor. Art itself is not redemptive;

art may very often make things much worse, for the artist at least; but the sudden shifting of point of view that allows for a restoration of sanity is often redemptive. There is an Updike who is forever being driven along dangerous narrow roads by a beautiful woman with an intriguing, because mysterious past, himself a hoarder of words, hoping only to experience transparency in the face of such wonder; there is another Updike in the guise of Reverend March, knowing his bitter metallic Calvinistic faith so unkillable that he may mock it, betray it, take every possible risk of damnation—because he is already saved, or already damned anyway. And out of this curious duality comes the paradoxical freedom of the true artist: having conquered both his temptation by vice and his temptation by virtue, he may live as ordinarily as anyone else.

The present-action of *The Centaur* is a long "dreaming-back" as Peter Caldwell, now a young adult, a painter who lives with his black mistress in a loft in New York City, tortures himself with doubts—*Was it for this that my father gave up his life?* In *Of the Farm* it is mentioned that George Robinson's death may have been hastened—but it is more his wife's fault, probably, than his son's; and in "Flight" it is the mother, eerily powerful, who insists upon the brilliant young boy's flight, his escape from that part of Pennsylvania in which she knows herself trapped, partly by the burden of her own aged but undying father. Yet though Peter worries about the role he may have played in exhausting his father, the novel as a whole works to liberate him from guilt and would be, for this reason alone, an unusual work for an American writer; O'Neill's *A Long Day's Journey into Night* is its exact reverse. The point is made explicitly that the father, in giving his life for others, enters a total freedom. He is the "noblest of all the Centaurs" and certainly the noblest of all the characters in Updike's now vast canvas: it is not Peter's right to doubt.

From George Caldwell's experience, then, comes a conviction that permeates Updike's work even when it appears in secularized and diminished settings —that one cannot assume any ultimate truths about other people, that they forever elude the word-nets we devise. Fearing he had cancer of the bowels, Caldwell had been more or less ready to die and (like Piet Hanema after the missile crisis) feels somewhat cheated after learning that his X-rays are clear, having been "spoiled" by the expectation of an end to his troubled life. Yet he accepts it all again. Life consists and will always consist of some version of Caldwell's lot:

> The prospect of having again to maneuver among Zimmerman and Mrs. Herzog and all that overbearing unfathomable Olinger gang made him giddy, sick; how could his father's seed, exploding into an infinitude of possibilities, have been funnelled into this, this para-

lyzed patch of thankless alien land, these few cryptic faces, those certain four walls of Room 204?

(Centaur)

Yet he accepts it. By doing so he is blessed with the release of death—he is freed of his ego, his concern for himself, and is liberated from the tyranny of the Calvinistic vision of life which his son cannot avoid inheriting. Peter, Prometheus and artist, a Dedalus as well who *must* rebel against so holy a fate in order to honor it, through his art, can encompass this wisdom only in the speculative recesses of his dreaming mind—he imagines his father as "saved," but he dares not accept such salvation for himself, because in giving his life to others (particularly to the mother who so blackmails him with her "love"), he cannot be an artist.

In assembling the short stories and sketches called, simply, *Olinger Stories*, Updike spoke of having said the "final word" in 1964; by having written *The Centaur* and transforming Olinger into Olympus, he closed the book of his own adolescence—the past is now a fable, receding, completed. But the past is never completed; it is not even *past*. It is a continual present. And so, having in a way immortalized and killed the "George Caldwell" of *The Centaur*, the author takes on, perhaps unconsciously, those traits he found so exasperating in the man as an adolescent: "Daddy, why are you so—superstitious? You make everything mean something it isn't. Why? Why can't you *relax*? It's so exhausting!" And he has taken on as well that remarkably detached, rather elegantly ego-less ability to glance without judgment on all sides of a melodramatic event, a basic clownishness, that seems to go largely unnoticed in his writing, but which gives it its energy, its high worth. Caldwell is funny, very funny, not with Bech's overwrought and neurotic wit, but with a fundamentally amiable acceptance of mystery. He reduces theological arguments to their basic emotional core and, correctly, presents it all as a cosmic joke: "What I could never ram through my thick skull was why the ones that don't have it [i.e., the non-Elect] were created in the first place. The only reason I could figure out was that God had to have somebody to fry down in Hell."

When the comic vision is weak in Updike's writing, a terrifying nihilism beckons: there is the skull behind the flesh, the skull's "nice" nostrils in Signorina Angeli's beautiful face, and the middle-aged weariness of *Rabbit Redux*. The truly religious imagination is never tragic, of course, and may be capable, as Flannery O'Connor is capable, of an ostensible cruelty that can alarm the liberal imagination because this cruelty is suggested as part of a cosmic joke. The pattern is always for compromise, for a scaling-down of passions, not even for tragic grandeur when it might be justified in a way by "the plot" —for everything is seen from an omniscient point of view, and that point of view is finally not human. When faith recedes or is lost, at once a half-consciously willed surrogate will appear, another form of desperation (as at the conclusion of *Couples* the socially conscious and "radical" younger generation of citizens is taking possession of Tarbox): if it is time-bound, historical rather than eternal, it carries with it the germ of its own disintegration. The process in time is always toward disintegration: the physical conquest of any embodiment of the life-giving Venus is a self-destructing act. And yet—"We love the flesh, its taste, its tones"— what to make of this torment except an art that, being totally transparent, submissive, finally achieves a kind of immortality?

Out of contradictory forces that, taken very seriously, have annihilated other writers or reduced them to fruitless angry quarrels in the guise of literary works, Updike has fashioned a body of writing that is as rich, mysterious, and infinitely rewarding as life itself—which, in fact, it *is*, finally claiming no intellectual or moral excuse for its own being. It is uniquely Updike's, and uniquely American. Updike exiled from America is unthinkable, and America without Updike to record it—unthinkable as well. His special value for us is his willingness to be disarmed of perspective, to allow his intensely realized worlds to flower with something of the mysterious effortlessness of nature itself, and to attempt to spiritualize the flesh since, for many in our time, the "flesh" may be all that remains of religious experience. The charge that Updike is too fascinated with the near-infinitesimal at the cost of having failed to create massive, angry works of art that more accurately record a violent time is unfair, because it is far more difficult to do what Updike does. Like Chiron/Caldwell, he accepts the comic ironies and inadequacies of ordinary life.

MARY ALLEN

John Updike's Love
of "Dull Bovine Beauty"

John Updike the writer is an honorable man. His heroes return to their wives in
the mellow atmosphere of appreciation and affection. His people do not kill or
maim or intentionally cause pain. After a few rebellious starts they adjust and
become at last like so many of us—comfortable. And for the woman who
would be anything more than a vegetable-wife, this writer is the cunning enemy
who would affectionately lull all womankind away from anything that has to do
with life of the mind or self-respect or the joy of doing to a more appropriate
and "natural" imbecility.

Perhaps Updike's horror of the powerful, manipulative mother turns him
with an extra fondness to the docile woman who can be dominated (and slept
with). Most of his women characters belong to one of these two opposing types,
each deadly in its way. Some readers see in Updike's women instead a wife-
whore division, but the wife and whore often resemble each other, wives acting
the part of whores and whores who are considered as possible wives. The mature
mother, however, exerting much the same influence as the dominant figures of
Kesey and Roth, is an overpowering presence in contrast to the pliable wives and
lovers. The difference for Updike's men is that they are much more successful at
escaping the mother than are the inmates of the Big Nurse and the son of Mrs.
Portnoy. The oedipal problem—a mother is someone you cannot sleep with—
for Updike seems to open the field to all others, a wide and delicious playground
for his men. Hardly a woman here is without sexual appeal. And everything can
be forgiven except frigidity.

From *The Necessary Blankness: Women in Major American Fiction of the Sixties.* © 1976
by the Board of Trustees of the University of Illinois. University of Illinois Press, 1976.

The story "Flight" clearly distinguishes between mother, who is to be feared, and girl (or wife), who is to be embraced. When Allen Dow was eleven or twelve his mother climbed with him to the top of a hill, dug her fingers into his hair, and announced that he was going to fly away from the small town below them where everyone else would stay forever. Her genius is "to give the people closest to her mythic immensity," and her boy is to be a phoenix. When Allen takes a liking to the plump, kindly Molly Bingaman, Mrs. Dow hysterically resists this hindrance to his flight, proclaiming that to go with a little woman (she might as well have said any woman) "puts you too close to the ground." Mrs. Dow's vulgar reference to "little hotpants" as part of her general attempt to denigrate sexual love for Allen, however, is a failure. He now knows, after being booed at a debate and using Molly's shoulder for comfort, the marvelous possibility of burying a "humiliation in the body of a woman," which is so revered by Updike's men. A woman's body may also be used for celebration. After winning a basketball game, Rabbit Angstrom makes love. When other skills are gone, the act of love is often the only means left by which to prove a victory.

The portrait of Mrs. Dow as the archetypal manipulative mother is complicated by her genuine desire for excellence, which, having no outlet in her own life, is channeled through Allen. Fortunately, since Mrs. Dow's dream is for the boy's flight, she allows Allen to escape. Giving up Molly, he admits defeat to his mother but is determined he shall never do so again. Updike's young men usually learn quite early in their lives the necessity of getting away from mother, both literally and, as best they can, emotionally. They do not generalize the fear of her into a fear of all women and find most others to be kind and comforting by comparison.

The women in "Flight" recall the account of the author's own life in "The Dogwood Tree: A Boyhood" when young John's mother forbids him to kiss his girlfriend, which only increases his desire to do so. The fondness of this boy— "My love for that girl carries through all those elementary-school cloakrooms" —is reflected in the creation of nearly all of Updike's male characters. What the young Allen Dow appreciates most about Molly is that she returns his love. She even comes running to him with her mother yelling at her to turn back. The Updike male is utterly vulnerable to such a woman's need for him, a dependence that is seen as unselfish and desirable. By contrast, the mother's need is always selfish. Mrs. Dow is indicted by omission as Allen reminisces that Molly "seems the one person who loved me without advantage."

Updike's young mothers are not of the same ilk as their elder, more dominant counterparts. Instead of controlling their children, they neglect them. When Janice Angstrom drowns her infant daughter she does so through alcoholic clumsiness, not as a result of an attempt to manipulate, which is the core of mother-hood in "Flight." Janice does not have the capacity to stand in as Harry's mother, or even to duplicate her own pettier but powerful mother. Updike does not so much suggest that mothers become more monstrous with age as that women of the past, holding more traditional values such as faith in religion and land, were stronger people. Irresponsibility and incompetence in motherhood replace the earlier ironhandedness, and while Updike shows weakness in his younger women, he is never so harsh on these gentle wives as he is on their powerful (and more interesting) mothers.

Chief among these is Mrs. Robinson in *Of the Farm*, probably Updike's most vivid woman and one of his best creations, a version of the mothers in "Flight," "Pigeon Feathers," and *Rabbit, Run*. Mrs. Robinson's verbal war with her daughter-in-law (by a second marriage) provides some of the most dramatic and realistic scenes in Updike's fiction. Joey Robinson dreads bringing his new wife to the farm, aware of the insidious power his mother is capable of exerting over both of them. Long before they get to her farmhouse Mrs. Robinson's image seems to spring out from it. Joey makes no attempt to rationalize what he considers his weakness in regard to his mother, but he complains bitterly to his wife Peggy that " 'I'm thirty-five and I've been through hell and I don't see why that old lady has to have such a hold over me. It's ridiculous. It's degrading.' "

The oedipal situation is clearly evident in the evening when Mrs. Robinson, the strap of her nightgown awry, waits while Joey takes Peggy up to her room, assuming that he will come back down to her. Later she condescendingly allows him to go to his wife's bed but equates the act with that of a dog: " 'Just give the dogs their water and take your wife to bed.' " The oedipal pattern is suggested in other cases where such a mother exists, on one occasion in *The Centaur* when George Caldwell's wife remarks that it is sad how " 'they don't allow men to marry their mothers.' " Angela Hanema of *Couples* half-jokingly claims that her husband sleeps with women when he is really trying to murder his mother. Joey Robinson's oedipal situation is compounded by his mother's lonely life on the farm and her neurotic and hysterical outbursts, one of them as she smashes plates in the kitchen after Joey's wife takes her place at the sink, and again on the way home from church when she screams uncontrollably.

To a degree Mrs. Robinson poses as a martyr, complaining that she is hated and let down by Joey, who left the farm and never became a poet as she had wished. But she accuses him (presumably all men) of perpetrating the erroneous idea that women like to suffer. She admits that her husband made possible the two things she wanted most, the farm and Joey, and claims that in return she granted Mr. Robinson his freedom. The fact that she assumes such a prerogative, and that she believes her husband did have his freedom (when he is so obviously shown to be trapped by the farm which was her way of life), is one instance of how Mrs. Robinson's concept of truth is merely a version of her own emotional needs.

At *Of the Farm*'s close Mrs. Robinson makes a pledge of a new freedom for her son. But it is difficult to believe she will allow such a freedom. On the other hand, Peggy—who enjoys possessing her husband and being possessed by him—because she is more easygoing, less distinguished by a personality, and above all because he is linked to her sexually, will be able to give him freedom. No wife in Updike's fiction *can* threaten the way a mother does. If he must, a man may replace his wife, but he has no control over his mother except in leaving her. Joey warns his mother not to poison his second marriage as she did the first, but it is unlikely that she would relinquish her power or that the couple could withstand her force if she tried to separate them.

The mother's strength is associated not only with an authoritarian family structure but with agrarian and religious values of the past, toward which Updike himself appears ambivalent. The mother's relationship to the past represents not only the literalness with which she is bound to a child's first years but the special value that tradition and nostalgia have for Updike. Mrs. Robinson is one of the last great characters before the world of Tarbox (*Couples*), in which no woman of her stature exists. As Hook pronounces in *The Poorhouse Fair*, "Women are the heroes of dead lands." While land is associated with the feminine, particularly the mother, the city is associated with the father. (Updike personally claims to be a man of middles, with his allegiance to his home town of Shillington, between country and city.)

Updike questions the return to the land, so often the symbolically virtuous journey, just as he questions the character of the dominant mother, so closely associated with it. Larry Taylor's excellent study of the pastoral and anti-pastoral themes in Updike's work shows a general progression from the more nostalgic and pastoral to the soundly anti-pastoral. Rabbit's flight to nature is the most obvious miscalculation of the healing power of nature, but Mrs. Robinson's mean-spirited attachment to land is another. In the story "Packed Dirt, Churchgoing, A Dying Cat, A Traded Car," it is the earth smoothed by feet that appeals to David Kern (and to Updike), a more humane soil than that of the farm.

Admittedly, land as a possession is satisfying. When Joey brings his new wife and stepson to the farm, he is proudly aware of how the vast acres he owns add to his stature. In lovingly describing his wife's body, another of his possessions, he refers to her as a fine piece of land: "My wife is wide, wide-hipped and long-waisted, and, surveyed from above, gives an impression of terrain, of a wealth whose ownership imposes upon my own body a sweet strain of extension; entered, she yields a variety of landscapes." Land associated with feminine sexuality is glorious indeed, but women rooted to the earth may use it as a prison for their husbands, men like Mr. Robinson and George Caldwell, who must escape to the city and to the classroom. Another such prisoner of the farm is Mr. Kern of "Pigeon Feathers," who finds no soul in the soil which only reminds him of death.

The mother is frequently linked with the idea of death. When Mrs. Robinson explains to Joey's stepson that tractors are like dying people, Joey realizes she is trying to sink into him "the hook of her death." As the giver of life, the mother assumes the right to destroy it, both literally and in the form of mental punishment. The association between mother and death is explicit in Updike's first novel, *The Poorhouse Fair*, in the name of the central female character, Amy Mortis. In "Pigeon Feathers" it is the authoritarian Mrs. Kern who commands that the beautiful pigeons be killed. The woman who gives life often balances it, through accident or design, with another child's death: Janice Angstrom gives birth to Nelson but accidentally kills her daughter June; Foxy Whitman (*Couples*), celebrated for her first pregnancy, terminates her second with abortion.

While mothers of an older generation are usually orthodox in religion, such as Mrs. Robinson, who would be strictly opposed to abortion, they usually lack true spirituality. Mrs. Robinson even admits she would not believe in God if she were forced to live in the city, and the discrepancy between her activities in church and her unchristian treatment of family is a further sign of the shallowness of her religious beliefs. Churchgoing, however, is not an automatic sign of hypocrisy. If a woman is responsive sexually, activity in a church may signify the addition of genuine spiritual qualities, which is the case for Foxy Whitman, the only churchgoing woman in Tarbox. By contrast, Angela Hanema, the non-churchgoer, is frigid and without spirituality. Updike is ambivalent in regard to the demise of traditional religious observances just as he is ambivalent about the value of land, seeing at the same time the beauty of traditions and the way they can become detrimental.

In his treatment of mothers Updike is on firm ground. His bitch mother represents little that is new to the type, but she is as effectively and as realistically drawn as anywhere in current fiction. Updike demonstrates with awareness and honesty not only the immense power such a woman has over her children but the mixed nature of her strength, which includes a potential that might have gone for good but instead is primarily destructive. Updike's male protagonists are as aware of the mother's potential to destroy as is the author, and for their benefit Updike presents wives who will soothe and comfort, but who are among the most dismal and hopelessly seduced beings to cross the pages of our literature. And in this case he is not entirely aware of his attitudes and of the way that they affect his fiction.

Updike makes a specific attempt to define his view of women in general in the title story of his collection *Museums and Women.* The narrator's view of his mother as "the index, inclusive and definitive of women," however, is contradicted by the woman he chooses for his wife, who does not faintly resemble his mother. The storyteller's mother, with her sense of his destiny (the true Updike mother), was the one who first brought him to the museum, pointing him in the direction of the great things of the past. The "pale creature" he meets at the top of the museum stairs, on the other hand, who is to become his wife, impresses him with the very opposite of that purposefulness. In this lost soul he sees "an innocent sad blankness where I must stamp my name." The museum with its valuable holdings of the past may be an apt metaphor for the mother with its emphasis on the qualities of "radiance, antiquity, mystery, and duty." But what does the young woman he meets here have to do with radiance, antiquity, mystery, or even duty? What truly entrances this visitor to the museum, however, does indeed apply only to this girl who is to become his wife: a statuette of a nude on a mattress. This figure (appropriately reclining in bed) is to him the most perfect item in the museum, a truly disturbing image of the desired woman, simply a marble object in a sexual posture.

The wives Updike creates are a sadly limited group, but their husbands like them well enough. The author has stated in an interview for *The Paris Review* that he never satirizes a character (the interview was before the publication of *Bech*), and he likewise never satirizes lovemaking, that favorite preoccupation of the fabulators. And writing in the broad tradition of manners, he shows women to be an indispensable part of society. Updike's men are particularly dependent upon them, and the first thing a man does when he leaves one woman (and he seldom leaves his wife permanently) is to find another, never considering the possibility of remaining alone.

Updike's most tender reverence is reserved for women's bodies. The elegant style with which he describes female anatomy often becomes overwrought, as his descriptions do generally. But it always conveys wonder. Even in the many explicit accounts of sexual activity, some of them ludicrous and even perhaps pornographic, there is an awe for the physical aspect of women. This form of adoration is far from a true consideration of women's needs, not taking into account their feelings and the consequences to them of sexual relations, but it is a kind of naive appreciation. Rabbit Angstrom boyishly begs Ruth to let him undress her and is delighted when she allows it. A special pause of wonder is observed before the lover approaches the woman's body. If a woman represents a return to the womb, as she does most memorably when Piet Hanema of *Couples* takes milk from his lover's breast, she bears only the remotest resemblance to the man's mother, who has long since ceased to give comfort or pleasure. The womb situation is often to be found only in running from mother, as Allen Dow runs to

Molly. In "Wife-Wooing," woman, womb, and wife are equated: "What soul took thought and knew that adding 'wo' to man would make a woman? The difference exactly. The wide w, the receptive o. Womb."

The very sight of women in the world gives a kind of grace to existence for Updike's men. A young grocery checker in "A & P" grows faint with delight as three girls in bathing suits come into the market. The loveliest girl, whose straps hang charmingly off her white shoulders, comes through his line and pays her bill with a dollar she produces from the top of her bathing suit. When the manager of the store blasphemously asks the girls to cover themselves, the checker, a martyr to their beauty, walks out on his much-needed job to protest the manager's action. A general appreciation for women is also shown, for example, by Piet Hanema, who might be speaking for all Updike men when he says he loves all the women he lies with.

Sexuality is far and away the most desirable trait in a woman, perhaps the only essential one. It is not necessarily associated with physical beauty. A woman in Updike may be remembered as pretty because of the fondness with which the love scenes are portrayed. But a close look at her features, which are usually given in detail, reveals that Ruth, for one, is marred by skin blemishes, a chunky body, and hair as multicolored as a dog's. Janice has thinning hair, tight dark skin, and a mouth that looks like a greedy slot. What endows these women with sexuality is rather an openness before men, a special and utter need for them, the lack of which makes someone like Angela Hanema, otherwise the most respected woman in Tarbox, unsatisfactory. Her husband sees her as "a lump, a barrier, a boarded door." Molly Bingaman, Janice Angstrom, Ruth Leonard, Vera Hummel, Peggy Robinson, Foxy Whitman, and Joan Maple of the Maple stories are all loved for their sexuality, the homely girls as well as the pretty ones. In fact, a case can be made that homeliness of a sort that makes women soft and vulnerable is in itself an attraction for Updike's men.

Of all his images of women, the one Updike paints most tenderly is the woman emerging from the tub or shower. Like Walker Percy's Binx Bolling (*The Moviegoer*), whose eyes sting with tears of gratitude for the beauty of his secretary's bottom as she passes to the water cooler, the heart of a Rabbit Angstrom grows rapturous at the sight of the steamy wife's or lover's behind. His first nostalgic memory of Janice after he leaves her is the way she comes from her bath, "doped and pleased with a little blue towel lazily and unashamed her bottom bright pink with hot water the way a woman was of two halves bending over and turning and laughing at his expression whatever it was." Vera Hummel makes her striking first appearance in *The Centaur* as she emerges from the high-school showers to the stunned delight of George Caldwell. Harry Conant in "The Wait" rhapsodizes over his lover Sally: "Though I live forever can I forget how I saw you step from a tub, your body abruptly a waterfall." It is not that lovemaking occurs with particular success in the shower (a favorite motif of the sixties), but that reverence is due the pristine loveliness of a woman just out of her bath.

A desire for the natural is a first concern with Updike's men, most noticeably with Rabbit. Without bothering about how Ruth might feel, he insists on rubbing the makeup from her face. This urge for the scrubbed nymph is an element of Updike's use of the pastoral as one way of idealizing women, primarily for the wonder of their bodies. But just as Rabbit's flights into nature to the orange groves of the south or to the hills of Mt. Judge offer neither solace nor escape, the homage to women's "purity" is often disastrous. When Rabbit insists on Ruth's "naturalness" and refuses to allow her to contaminate herself with contraceptives, she must bear the consequences of an unwanted pregnancy. The thought of a pastoral retreat may suggest a luscious escape, as it does in "The Wait" when the lovers, stranded in a Washington, D.C., airport, fantasize a life together in faraway Wyoming. But they are soon jolted back to the problems of their mundane love affair. Updike's anti-pastoralism eventually overwhelms the pastoral ideal.

Both as a pastoral ideal and as part of a tradition depicted by Denis de Rougemont that love in the Western world exists only when an obstacle is present, creating a triangular situation, Updike's characters yearn for the unattainable. In a review of *Love in the Western World* which describes the conflict in the West between passion and marriage, Updike agrees that "love as we experience it *is* love for the Unattainable Lady" (a statement in which Updike characteristically assumes that his male viewpoint is the definitive one). This lady is a form which takes on the male lover's own spirit. For Updike, with his particular fixation on the past, this may mean that "a woman, loved, momentarily eases the pain of time by localizing nostalgia; the vague and irrecoverable objects of nostalgic longing are assimilated, under the pressure of libidinous desire, into the details of her person." A particularly good example of the way this works is in "The Persistence of Desire," one of Updike's finest stories. Clyde Behn, visiting his home town, meets a former girlfriend in the dentist's office and immediately approaches her with passionate attentions, which to her are ridiculous. The emotion that engulfs him is a nostalgia for the youthful self he was when he first knew her, an image now favorably tinged by time. The only value of her existence is in her connection with him. Like most Updike women she is merely practical, not only lacking the sense of nostalgia herself but altogether missing it in anyone else. Such women are entirely without the nuances of feeling which enhance the Updike hero and make him more complex than the heroine. It is Clyde's glory to add to this woman's bareness: "Except for the interval of himself —his splendid, perishable self—she would never see the light."

The bachelor Bech is one who, after years of deifying women, locates the ideal in a Bulgarian poetess. For him she is quite unattainable—foreign, independent, complete—noticeably unlike any American woman in Updike's work and his only woman, idealized or otherwise, who is given qualities, other than sexual, which are superior. It is not only distance that lends to the Bulgarian's appeal and distinction, although we realize Bech's weakness for her unattainability. She is truly an accomplished person. Apparently it would not occur to Updike to attribute any American woman with the talent and wisdom he grants to this individual. In all Bech's loves there had been an urge to rescue, to impress with his own character, but this foreign poetess needs nothing. Not even a husband. Bech admits that in America "you must be very uncharming not to marry," which is quite the way Updike portrays the American culture. Bech is a rare bachelor, one of the few single persons in Updike's fiction who is not completely alienated from society. He is not as distasteful as the women who do not marry, but his failure to do so becomes the butt of satire.

Updike's men do yearn for the unattainable, but he is finally much committed to a concept of realism and draws his characters away from their dreams into life much closer to the way it is lived in suburban America. Americans do marry often, and marriage is his topic. With full attention to its difficulties and disillusionments, Updike shows marriage to be the inevitable testing ground in contemporary life. Even the protagonist of "The Hermit" (not a typical subject for Updike) is routed from his forest retreat, after being visited there by a woman and shown the failure of his attempt to live alone. Updike's characters think so much in terms of marriage that when Rabbit spends one night with the prostitute Ruth he refers to it as their wedding night and to her as his wife.

The marriage commitment is shaky, as most people falter toward divorce, but it stands. There is good reason, other than moralistic or traditional, however, why people usually do not divorce. Updike's wives are so similar and interchangeable (unless they are frigid, and most of them are not) that divorce would serve little purpose. Bech, for whom the Bulgarian poetess is unique, admits that other women all share the trait of "narrowly missing an undisclosed prototype." The monotonous affairs of *Couples* show a general malaise which cannot be corrected by changing partners, although out of boredom switches occur frequently on a temporary basis. Only Piet and Foxy, considered to be the true lovers, divorce, so that they may marry each other. But soon they will become just another couple. The same sense of the tired exchange of partners occurs in "The Witnesses," the story of a man who brings a second wife to visit friends who remark on her resemblance to the first wife. The only valid reason for leaving a wife is apparently frigidity, as is the case with Angela Hanema.

The families that stay together usually do so without the aid of particularly dramatic events, but Updike sees them through in a lifelike way that is based on a closer look at suburbia than many critics of such an existence are willing to give. In an appreciative study of American writers of the last two decades, Tony Tanner observes that while most American novelists consider middle-class life a "desert of unreality," Updike shows it to be more complex than is usually admitted. He has the nerve to accept suburban life as the place where contemporary American characters "will learn what they learn and lose what they lose." It is rare to find an American author who writes from inside the establishment and with so little reliance on acts of violence. In Updike's fiction terrible events pass across television screens like mirages while the bewildered souls of the sixties sit helplessly back and watch. When asked about the infrequent use of violence in his work, while it inundates us in the news and in literature, Updike says his reason for showing it so rarely in his writing is that there has been so little of it in his life.

It is Updike's approach to normalcy that gives some credence to his picture of women, even the dullest ones, whom it would be tempting to believe are only a creation of his male chauvinism. He appears not to be fully aware of the extent to which he demeans the female character, and surely his heroines are not representative of enterprising women who contradict the theory of women's blankness. But the type he represents may be defended as one which exists in significant enough numbers to be a crucial factor in American life.

Updike gives us the dreary aspects of the housewife's existence through the lyricism of his male point of view. This stylistic quality makes the reading of Updike at times enjoyable while it soothes the reader away from the fact that from a woman's viewpoint no such lyricism in describing her life would be possible. In depicting the mundane subject with a lyrical style Updike suggests that marriage itself combines these elements in a story like "Wife-Wooing," where a husband labors as any other lover might to stir his lady's desire. The *wife*, who may be as distasteful as Janice is at the beginning of *Rabbit, Run*, where marriage is a system of constraints, is not, however, essentially a distasteful concept to Updike's men. A wife is the comfort they seek. Their truest entrapment is never more to their wives than to themselves, and even a possessive wife can be a liberating force. Pastoral lyricism is thus by no means limited to praise of the unattainable lady. The speaker of "Wife-Wooing" poetically relates: "I wed wide warm woman, white-thighed. Wooed and wed. Wife. A knife of a word that for all its final bite did not end the wooing. To my wonderment." The seven years of marriage have brought the couple no distance, only "to the same trembling point, of beginning," a statement more in praise of marriage's mysterious possibility for regeneration than an indictment of the union. Most couples in Updike's fiction continue to work for some unnameable goal which makes their lives if not extraordinary at least worth living.

Updike's lyricism in behalf of the female body and his devotion to the idea of marriage, however, depend upon an idea of the undeniably *stupid* woman. The classic statement of the Updike male regarding the Updike female (as wife, not mother) is made by Peter Caldwell (*The Centaur*), who says of Iris Osgood, "I was tired and wanted only to pillow my head on her low I.Q." Iris is a future Updike wife, appealing to both boys and to men as she sits "immersed in dull bovine beauty." Zimmerman, the principal of the school, fondles her arm as the class proceeds. For Peter she is "one of those dull plain girls who was totally unfashionable in the class and yet with whom I felt a certain inner dance." She has the sexuality first in the heart of the Updike male, and at a young age, as will be the case later on, her moronic niceness is the comfort men need, especially gentle, insecure men like Peter, his father, and Rabbit Angstrom, whose egos are so delicate that they must be insured by a superiority over women. In turning from the strong, feared mothers, Updike's men ask little more than a safe, warm place—precisely, a woman's body. Updike is, of course, too realistic to show marriage as a state of easy peace, for even with relatively uncomplicated people it is often tense and difficult. But calm is more likely to result in ennui than to erupt in violence. And the result to the Updike male who has chosen a woman who will not threaten his limited intelligence is a boredom far beyond the normal expectations of daily existence. The dramatic clashes of will that exist for older couples are replaced by the repetitious irritations that plague the couples of Rabbit's generation. The younger wife is simply too bland to be capable of an interesting confrontation, which is one reason why marriages endure.

There is nothing subtle in Updike's qualification of his women as "dumb." Rabbit shouts the word when he runs from Janice. And Ruth is very little brighter, with her bad grammar and her conventional and crude ideas. In "Giving Blood" Richard Maple says of his wife Joan that her "stupidity I don't mind." Their marriage problems, characteristically, are sexual. A whole classroom of unintelligent girls confront George Caldwell. Judy Lengel, a classmate of Iris Osgood, cannot begin to understand the questions she is asked about geology, let alone answer them. She is as "dumb as pure white lead." Caldwell tells her that after the quiz she can forget all about it—soon she will be married with six kids. His remark to Peter after the girl goes laments not her lack of intelligence but the fact that "her father'll have an old maid on his hands." Peter Caldwell's girlfriend Penny is lyrically referred to as "my Penny, my little dumb, worried Penny. Suddenly, thickly, I loved her," the proximity of the statements suggesting a strong causal relationship between her being dumb and his loving her. In "Flight" three bright young girls are "disfigured by A's as if by acne," an equation of intelligence and ugliness. Another case of the preferred stupid woman is Joey Robinson's choice of Peggy as his second wife. His mother cleverly attacks him by pointing out how surprising it is that the boy Richard is bright, because the mother is not. She tells Joey she is ashamed that he would need a stupid woman to give him confidence. He admits that his wife is stupid but that it does not matter to him. The rejected wife was brighter but not as sensual as wife number two.

Despite the way he depicts women, Updike claims that his novels "are all about the search for useful work. So many people these days have to sell things they don't believe in, and have jobs that defy describing." A person must build his life outward from a job. For Rabbit to demonstrate kitchen items or to sell used cars is pitiful, especially in view of his former glory on the basketball court. What makes Piet Hanema superior to the other residents of Tarbox (along with his virility) is an almost spiritual feeling for his work as an architect of fine traditional houses. George Caldwell, the bedraggled teacher who presumably hates his job, actually invests it with a magic that is not lost on his heathenish students. His charisma in the classroom is Updike's way of showing him to be a superior and a good man.

But if the novels are about the search for useful work, what about work for women? Updike's statement includes a sympathetic comment on the occupation of housewives whose lives show a terrible sense of emptiness. And yet not only does he fail to suggest anything better for them—he will not *allow* it. None of his women consider meaningful jobs, although they are equally if not more dissatisfied with their petty lives than their husbands are with theirs. Even if childbearing were fulfilling to women, and there is no indication in this fiction that it is, it offers nothing for the middle and later years. And yet Updike equates childbirth for a woman with a career for a man: in Tarbox, where everyone has to some degree lost his soul, "the men had stopped having careers and the women had stopped having babies." In this "post-pill paradise," the fallen state of Eden, birth control is a form of sin. But the way Updike's women react to their children is also a form of sin. Mothers of the past painfully dominate their children; younger mothers neglect theirs. Sterility, however, is disliked so intensely by the men of Tarbox that the infertile Bea Guerin claims that men actually injure her because they cannot impregnate her. (She becomes slightly more acceptable when she decides to adopt a baby.) Angela is at fault for never giving her husband a son. Reproduction is important primarily as a way of establishing male virility, not because of any intrinsic value attributed to the child or to the woman who carries the child.

Aside from lovemaking and childbearing, there is almost nothing for Updike's women to do. Piet Hanema is appalled at the housewife's measly chores, but it never occurs to him that any of his lovers would be doing much during the day besides waiting for his visit. (Presumably the men still go to work between lovemaking episodes.) The only career women Updike portrays, aside from a pitiful secretary or two, are prostitutes, who do much the same work as the wife or lover. Perhaps he simply cannot imagine what a woman might want to do other than minister to a man's needs! Bech's question to a lady friend, "What do you do?," which he retracts as stupid, would be an unfortunate one to ask any of Updike's women. Bech's conclusion, which seems to be voicing Updike's own view, is that "merely to rise each morning and fill her skin to the brim with such loveliness was enough for any woman to do." If this statement is intended to be humorous it is much too close to an attitude in the non-satirical works to be identified as such.

Updike's women not only lack involving work of their own, but they are too dull to be interested in what their husbands do, making only the most perfunctory inquiries. In "Toward Evening" a young man in New York arrives home from work in good spirits with an expensive present for his younger daughter. His wife is irritated with the gift and with him for not answering her ritual question about his work day; but her mood is considered quite "understandable in view of her own confined existence." The young wife in "Ace in the Hole" (the germ of *Rabbit, Run*) taunts her husband when he loses his job by asking what he will do next: " 'Go back to the Army? Your mother? Be a basketball pro?' " A wife humiliates her husband by comparing his past achievements with the mediocrity of his present condition, understandably equating it with her own. Ace's wife ridicules the very possibility of a meaningful occupation; it does not exist for her (she has a nondescript office job), and his ambitions appear ridiculous. Suggesting that women miss out on a world of things by not being athletes, Ace laments that their daughter, who has the hands of a natural, will never be able to use them. " 'Baby, we got to have a boy.' " Ace (now referred to as Fred) knows he could be doing something better than parking cars for a living. It is not surprising that he is soon fired for smashing one of them.

Waiting at home is the archetypal Updike wife, Janice Springer Angstrom —vulnerable, sexual, good-natured, and stupid. She makes a striking image, this housewife of 1960, mesmerized in front of the TV, drinking an old-fashioned and watching the Mouseketeers. Her pregnancy hardly suggests the great gift of life as she sags inertly into her chair. Both Janice and the prostitute Ruth, as Gerry Brenner points out, represent the ultimate "natural" state. They do nothing and are reduced to mere vegetables. Janice's physical vegetation reflects a thorough mental vegetation. In contrast to graceful Rabbit, who has just come from shooting a perfect basket as he was able to do in high school, she is noticeably clumsy. Arriving at home, Rabbit is confronted by the absence of all grace and the presence of mere clutter, of which Janice is a part. The only light in the room comes from the TV, which she once nearly smashed by getting tangled in the cord. His means of response to this mess is to carefully unfold his own coat and neatly hang it up.

The Angstrom marriage is far from a success, but there are no dramatic, bitter battles. The couple simply drag along through years of tedious irritations. In appearance Janice is neither beautiful nor downright ugly, just small, a woman "with a tight dark skin, as if something swelling inside is straining against her littleness. . . . Her eyes dwindle in their frowning sockets and her little mouth hangs open in a dumb slot." Her passivity is overwhelming. She cannot even care for her child, who has been taken, appropriately, to the more capable Mother Angstrom. Janice relies heavily on her own mother (whom she dislikes) as well, one more sign of weakness. Rabbit is in no way fond of her mother either, but a mother-in-law can never be in the class of a mother. Rabbit sees Mrs. Springer as something comic. His own mother is the one person in life whom he fears, despite others who have reason to consider him an enemy.

Rabbit's world consists of a pattern of nets and other constrictions to be escaped. When he comes home the door is locked on his domestic trap. But at the moment, at least, he is on the *outside* of that trap, enlightened enough to understand its ugliness and to attempt a retreat. Viewed from the inside, which Updike is not inclined to do, the locked door suggests much more of a trap for Janice than it does for Rabbit. She has no idea how the door got locked; it "just locked itself." Only after Rabbit runs away is Janice forced to consider altering her life, and then the only possibilities are pitifully based on the simplest abso-lutes: she will get a divorce and be like a nun, or her husband will come back and love her. She may be too pitiful to elicit much compassion, and if she is only a caricature created to illustrate Updike's concern with the banal, she is not worth serious discussion. But Janice may be all too representative of a great many housewives sitting dully behind closed doors.

Janice first met Harry Angstrom when they both held dreary jobs in Kroll's department store, work which they and the other employees hated. Years later Rabbit's work has not improved much as he demonstrates MagiPeel Peelers in five-and-dime stores, a trifling occupation for a man, so close to the trivia of housework. We are made very aware that he must have talents for something better. Even tending Mrs. Smith's garden is an improvement. But what about Janice? Our author never allows us to *expect* her to do anything important or interesting. On the Mouseketeer show Janice is watching when Rabbit comes home, Jimmy, the big Mouseketeer, delivers this message: " 'God wants some of us to become scientists, some of us to become artists, some of us to become firemen and doctors and trapeze artists. And He gives to each of us the special talents to become these things, *provided we work to develop them.* We must *work*, boys and girls. So: Know Thyself. Learn to understand your talents, and then work to develop them. That's the way to be happy.' " Trite as the message sounds, the idea is not far from Updike's own stated feelings about the impor-tance of significant work. The TV program presents the message effectively to children, and the Mouseketeer intrigues Rabbit, who is interested in his sales pitch. The subject of using one's talents, too, is particularly timely to Rabbit in his current struggle with his unchallenging life.

But what impact does the message have for Janice, who is the person at home watching the show? As far as we can see she has no talents (even the hot dogs she prepares are split and twisted). The vocations mentioned by the Mouseketeer are obviously those traditionally followed by men. And if she were to know herself as he suggests, what would she find? What encouragement is there for her to emerge from her stupor? Rabbit is aware of the image his company tries to present of the housewife, and he kiddingly reminds his wife of it. She is *supposed* to look tired, because she *is* a housewife. She does look tired, but not from a day's work—just from doing nothing. Rabbit seems sympathetic, but neither he nor Janice can imagine other possibilities for her. It is never suggested that *she* run away.

Janice epitomizes the trait most prominent in the Updike wife: stupidity. "There seems no escaping it: she is dumb." Updike uses the word *dumb* consistently in reference to young women, although few are as dumb as poor Janice. One way of defining such stupidity is if a woman is unable to grasp the meaning of a man's jokes. Rabbit tries to tease Janice into seeing what he does with the image of the housewife by relating his work to her. When she does not laugh he considers her to be stupid. His humor, of course, is not funny to her. She vaguely senses but does not truly comprehend the unfortunate parallels between her husband's work and her own life. Neither women nor men are expected to be highly intelligent in Updike's world, but his women lack even the merest awareness of complexity, seeing things in simplistic absolutes as both Janice and Ruth do. Rabbit's skill has been primarily athletic (in contrast to women's physical awkwardness), but beyond that he does imagine that there is some better "thing" out there, a perception none of the women have.

In their stupidity the women become alike. When Ruth tells Rabbit that Tothero's girlfriend is "dumber than you can know," he says that he does know because he is married to her twin. A wife may be unique in her association with a particular man, but there is little else to distinguish her. The male wishes to impress his identity on the female's blankness, but she is often so blank that little impression can be made. Rabbit dreams that Janice is weeping for something his mother did, and "to his horror her face begins to slide, the skin to slip slowly from the bone, but there is no bone, just more melting stuff underneath." There is no identity to hold Janice together. He tries futilely to catch the melting stuff in his hands and form it into something complete.

Janice, like nearly every Updike woman, is a sexual creature. Rabbit fondly recalls how they first made love in a friend's apartment after work. They were married when she was pregnant, an instigating factor in many Updike marriages but one having little to do with their ultimate mediocrity. When Janice comes home from the hospital with their second child, Rabbit is again obsessed with making love to her. When she refuses him because it is too soon after giving birth, he runs from her a second time. Janice, who is not frigid, would not ordinarily have abstained from lovemaking. But this one refusal turns out to be a fatal mistake.

Like most Updike women, Janice is good-natured in her sexuality, combining qualities we rarely find linked in female characters in American literature. The undramatic virtue of geniality can be easily passed over in light of Janice's more obvious limitations. But certainly good-naturedness such as hers is one reason why many marriages survive as well as they do. Janice is affectionately forgiving when Rabbit comes to her in the hospital during the period when he is living with Ruth. In her limited way she loves him, and he always answers back, "I love *you*," somehow making it sound convincing at the moment. For her loyalty and affection Janice merits affection in return, but her meagerness of soul is incapable of inspiring great love (which is probably not possible for any of Updike's people). Rabbit, who at least envisions some kind of grandeur, laments to Tothero that the " 'little thing Janice and I had going, boy, it was really second-rate.' "

After Rabbit runs from Janice, the only person she can look to for help is her mother, an unfortunate choice, for the contact is always demeaning. "There was always that with Mother the feeling she was dull and plain and a disappointment, and she thought when she got a husband it would be all over, all that." (Rabbit's mother also belabors Janice's incompetence, attributing her only with the skill necessary to trap a husband.) Rabbit and Janice are made primarily responsible for their baby's death, but Mrs. Springer is also partially responsible. It is immediately after she phones Janice, discovering that Rabbit has gone again and insisting on coming over immediately, that her daughter is panicked into cleaning up her house and her baby and the accident in the bathtub occurs. Mrs. Springer does not visit her daughter to help but to make fun of her because she cannot keep her husband. And Janice, already self-consciously aware of her inadequacy, tragically demonstrates it by accidentally drowning her child.

Updike rarely considers a woman's point of view. But both Janice and Ruth are shown on occasion through interior monologues, Ruth's being reminiscent of Molly Bloom's as she recalls in detail her many sexual experiences. Janice's simple mind dwells with little new insight on the crisis in her life, but there is pathos in her lonely confusion. We now begin to see the effects on her of continually being considered stupid. In her own mind she makes a sensible defense for herself which she would probably never have the confidence to announce to her husband effectively: "Here he called her dumb when he was too dumb to have any idea of how she felt." Rabbit admittedly is not interested in how she feels, for the important thing, he says, is how *he* feels. Surely one reason for Janice's ineptness is the image of her that is set by others. Her consciousness of not being understood, which is shown no place outside of this one interior monologue, is as poignant as it is unexpected: "That was what made her panicky ever since she was little this thing of nobody knowing how you felt and whether nobody could know or nobody cared she had no idea." Only with this rare insight into Janice do we begin to imagine the lonely horror she must feel—to be clumsy, slow, and "dumb," to be referred to constantly in such a way, and then, in a drunken daze, to bring about the death of her own child.

Rabbit, however, does have valid motivation to run from Janice. She *is* disgusting, and he is all too aware that there is something better than his limited life with her. Thus, we would expect him, in turning to another woman as he naturally does, to look for superior qualities not found in Janice. But again he opts for inferiority. Some readers see his affair with Ruth as a love match. But it is merely another sexual adventure for Rabbit, and when the involvement demands that he consider her welfare, he runs from her as he runs from everything else. Ruth is somehow sexually appealing to Rabbit, but not outstanding in any other way. She is far from beautiful, and yet her coarseness rather attracts him; she may be overweight, but he says she is "not *that* fat. Chunky, more . . . her thighs fill the front of her dress so that even standing up she has a lap. Her hair, kind of a dirty ginger color, is bundled in a roll at the back of her head." From her plumpness Rabbit deduces that she is good-natured (a thought process Updike frequently employs, just as he concludes that sexual women must be stupid). The morning after his first night with Ruth he finds her homeliness pitiful, something he had not noticed the evening before. The lack of beauty never daunts the Updike lover, however. Rabbit comes back for more, drawn on by Ruth's limitations and her need for him, running toward the very things he claimed were unbearable in his marriage.

For Rabbit to prove that he is a winner he needs women like Janice and Ruth. Only their incapacity can confirm his superiority. To explain his mediocre golf game he replaces thoughts of his own inadequacy with the concept of women's stupidity: "In his head he talks to the clubs as if they're women. The irons, light and thin yet somehow treacherous in his hands, are Janice. *Come on, you dope, be calm. . . . Oh, dumb, really dumb.*" Like Janice, Ruth is "dumb," which is just the quality to appeal to Rabbit. When he finds her reading a book he taunts her by saying there is no need for her to read when she has him. A woman immobile is a delight to such a man; Ruth is a "perfect statue, un-adorned woman, beauty's home image" (the image developed in "Museums and

Women"). When she speaks, however, the image is spoiled as her crude expressions spill forth. When Tothero, Rabbit's former coach, claims that he develops his athletes' three tools—head, body, and heart—she quickly adds, "the crotch." When Ruth is not immobile, like Janice she is uncoordinated—an awkward bowler, a bloated and a lazy swimmer—while Rabbit continues to regard himself as the graceful athlete. His concepts are lyrical and ideal in contrast to the practical, dull thoughts that enter the heads of his women. Life for them holds no quest of higher things, no sense of the meaningful ambiguities which make Rabbit a more interesting character than they have the possibility of being.

For Updike to consider the "dreams" of his women characters is something of a parody, although he claims that he never satirizes. When Rabbit reminisces about his glory as a basketball star, which he frequently refers to in his conversation with Ruth, she admits to her dream of wanting to be a great cook. This accomplishment would presumably distinguish her from the inadequate Janice, whose lamb chops are greasy. But in fact Ruth has become a good eater, not a good cook. Her culinary skill is given a test only in the preparation of hot dogs, which she can indeed cook without splitting them open as Janice does. When Rabbit first asks Ruth, "What do you do?," that question terrible to so many women, she answers the familiar "Nothing." She can hardly reply that she is a prostitute, although the lowly state of whore, as Ruth later points out, is not really unlike that of other women. Rabbit is aware of this and declines to use the word *prostitute* in reference to Ruth unless it is used for every woman who is not married. Categorizing all unmarried women this way, however, which is meant to elevate Ruth, only results in denigrating all unmarried women. Married women, if not referred to as prostitutes, are often treated as such. When Rabbit attempts to make love to his wife after she has had her baby, demanding that she "roll over," she points out to him that he treats her like a prostitute.

Janice appears as a hopelessly limited being throughout *Rabbit, Run*, but ten years later in *Rabbit Redux* her life is surprisingly on the upswing. As if to be fair (Updike does not support a double standard of morality), it is her turn for a love affair, and she finds Charlie Stavros while working part-time at her father's car lot. In the last ten years her smallness has hardened into a leaner, better figure, and she has discovered the joy of sex, the one thing a person is made for, which she feels Rabbit locked up for her through the years. As she becomes more active physically, if not mentally, Rabbit grows fatter, slower, and more conservative politically. His response to women has not basically changed, but he is tiring. He admits that "all this fucking . . . just makes me too sad." *Rabbit Redux* ends with Rabbit and Janice in a motel room, falling asleep without making love, either as a weary resignation to their unexciting marriage or with a new emphasis for Updike on the platonic. (His attitudes elsewhere make it difficult to believe the latter.) In either case, the Angstrom marriage is more solid than ever as Janice proves to be Harry's true mate.

Even though a dramatic change has apparently taken place in Janice, the effects are demonstrated primarily when she is not with her husband. Her adventures do little to change his former concept of her. A new vitality results from her love affair, which splits them apart for a time, but Janice's dowdy familiarity predominates as the affair dies and she comes back to Harry. Changed as he might be by living with Jill and Skeeter, a teenage girl and her Negro friend, he has not changed about "dumb" Janice. He is surprised by her affair, amazed that she could appeal to anyone but him: " 'Who'd have that mutt?' " a comment not necessarily meant to be nasty but uttered as a mere statement of fact. And yet it is assumed that all the women involved with Harry love him and want him. He is not joking when he remarks of Janice, " 'At her age, are you supposed to have a good time?' " Harry's conviction that another man could not be deeply interested in Janice is borne out as Updike sees to it that Stavros tires of Janice. When she returns to Harry, still charming as she emerges from the shower, we are reminded that this is the familiar, clumsy Janice as she cuts herself several times while shaving her legs in the bathtub.

Updike's attempt to give Janice a new image, while retaining her basic stupidity, is unsuccessful. He is unable to allow her the capacity or even the good luck for any significant changes. Her way of expressing a new sense of self is artificial and trite: " 'It's the year nineteen sixty-nine and there's no reason for two mature people to smother each other to death simply out of inertia. I'm searching for a valid identity and I suggest you do the same.' " Rabbit recognizes that any ideas she might have picked up all come from her new lover. The attempt to be witty or topical only reveals her lack of intelligence in a clearer light. Stavros comes to recognize Janice's inadequacy, but at least, as she relates to Harry, " 'he never told me how dumb I am, every hour on the hour like you do.' " This quality so predominates in Harry's thoughts of her that when he learns of her love affair his first reaction is not one of shock or hurt but a repetition of the familiar adjective: "You dumb bitch." When he and Stavros later discuss the situation which Harry has passively accepted, he says, " 'So now you've tried her in all positions and want to ship her back. Poor old Jan. So dumb.' " This is not the outburst of bitterness or a ploy to get Stavros to give her up, but merely his customary remark. One of the rare compliments he directs to Janice, given while he makes love to Jill, poorly, is in combination with the insulting epithet: " 'My poor dumb mutt of a wife throws a better piece of ass backwards than you can manage frontwards.' " Stupidity in a woman is as ever linked with her sexuality in the mind of the Updike male.

Stavros is affected by Janice's stupidity when he has some kind of attack and calls on her to get his pills. The bathroom door sticks (the clumsy Janice); she cannot find the light cord (the incompetent Janice); and then it takes time for her eyes to become accustomed to the dark (the slow Janice). Finally, when she brings the wrong pills Charlie tells himself, "Harry is right. She is stupid." In her panic she is genuinely concerned about him, but her good will never makes the dramatic impact that is made by her incapacity. As Charlie writhes on the bed, she "very stupidly lets the faucet water run to get cold." Janice, in desperation, recalls Harry's telling her she has the touch of death. Her only instinct, which proves to be the right one, is to press herself against Charlie, as if in the act of love. His spasm passes, and she feels that the mark of death on her has been lifted. Her warmth and sexuality in this case outweigh the stigma of her stupidity.

Janice's sexual coming of age is her salvation. Rabbit once left her because she would not make love, and she will not commit such an error again. She is redeemed from the greatest sin (which she only committed once) — failure in bed. Harry does want her back, which is obvious to everyone who knows him. Now the score has been evened, which seems the real motivation on Updike's part for Janice's affair. While she genuinely needs rejuvenation, the Janice of *Rabbit, Run* is not capable of seeking it. Only Rabbit has the nerve to run. But if anything is to happen to her it must be a sexual affair, for this is the only valid experience Updike can imagine for a woman. And being the utterly dependent woman she is, Janice places her whole sense of identity with Stavros just as she once did with Rabbit. Updike's men never become so involved with particular women, nor do their quests end with them. His heroes continue to seek something higher in work, athletics, or a vague spirituality. In a sense they go through women to find their higher selves, while a person like Janice finds what she values in Harry or Stavros specifically.

Janice's lover soon tires of her, and she returns from her affair mellowed but not buoyed up. More dependent on Harry than ever, she now knows that no one else will have her. The return to him comes about with none of the style she was beginning to show when she left. Once again she is dowdy Janice, properly humbled and inept. If *Rabbit Redux* is indicative, Updike's wife of the future will be as bound in her limitations as ever. Janice is again the wife of *Rabbit, Run*:

> Janice gets out of the driver's seat and stands beside the car looking
> lumpy and stubborn in a charcoal-gray loden coat he remembers
> from winters past. He had forgotten how short she is, how the dark
> hair has thinned back from the tight forehead, with that oily shine
> that puts little bumps along the hairline. She has abandoned the
> madonna hairdo, wears her hair parted way over on one side, unflat-

teringly. But her mouth seems less tight; her lips have lost the crimp in the corners and seem much readier to laugh, with less to lose, than before. His instinct, crazy, is to reach out and pet her—do something, like tickle behind her ear, that you would do to a dog; but they do nothing.

Janice as the family pet—mindless, dependent, cuddly—is exactly what Harry wants. He announces to her that in his affections she ranks third in the family, after their son Nelson and after his own mother. When Janice and Harry meet again after their separation, her suggestion that they go to a motel gives her the shabby sense of a pickup, not the acceptability of a wife. At the Safe Haven Motel Harry signs up for the room while she waits in the car like "some dubious modern product extravagantly wrapped, in a metal package rich with waste space." When he motions for her to show the suitcase to the desk clerk and she does not understand, he exclaims in the familiar way, " 'God, she's dumb!' "

The strength of *Rabbit Redux* is the natural way it links with the Angstroms of ten years earlier, not by illustrating sweeping developments of character but by showing how people continue in their habits. It is expected that Janice will return to her husband and that he will desire her for the same reasons he always has, which are emphasized now by time and familiarity. Approaching middle age and disillusioned by their quests, the Angstroms accept what is comfortable. Janice's love affair may have awakened her to a degree, but it only reinforces Harry's custom of condescending to his inferior.

It is quite credible that Harry would live out his life with a Janice, but his liaison with Jill, the eighteen-year-old waif who lives with him for a time, is a less believable and more doomed combination. As a younger man, Harry had the Updike tenderness for all women, especially for those who were not beautiful but who were easygoing and sexual. He is now unable to be warm to someone like Jill, a new kind of girl in a new age. He sees her as being all dried up sexually, and while he continues to make love to her, their lovemaking is a dismal experience. With her, the wonder he previously felt for women is gone. Because of their age difference he at first appears as the protective father, but her apparent sophistication and wildly foreign way of life harden him to the possibilities of being close to her. He is anything but protective. Her form of dependence is not the open vulnerability he is used to, and her toughness makes him impotent.

When Jill first comes home with Harry they bathe together, at her request. The sight of the woman in her bath, a favorite of Updike men, in Jill's case fails to create the usual awed response. Even after bathing she never seems quite clean enough, not being plump and pink like the others but lean and hard and gray.

Harry notes with disappointment, as she does, that he is not sexually aroused with her, a failure which is not merely the result of fatigue. His characteristic virility is evident during the same period with the less attractive, alcoholic, and vulnerable Peggy Fosnacht, a neighbor and friend of Janice. There is nothing to do but kiss that woman and then make love to her, which Harry does with his customary skill and pleasure, coming partially from the thought of what he is giving to her. She is the blank check, like most women, "blank until you fuck her," a concept he attributes to Skeeter but which is a version of his own. Jill lacks a kind of animal succulence that brings out what chivalry Harry is capable of. She is sadly aware of her failure to arouse men—Harry is not the first. From the moment he notes his impotence with her he shows a marked coolness to Jill which he has never before demonstrated, even to the most vulgar or simple woman.

We are led to believe that Harry's coolness to Jill is a result of an attitude toward her wealth. He is angry at this "rich bitch" for "calling his living room tacky," and he notes with scorn that the money spent for her Porsche, now in disrepair, could support a whole family of less extravagant people. But such materialism has never been an obsession with Rabbit, to whom the clutter and banality, not precisely the poverty, of his middle-class life are the focus of *Rabbit, Run.* He can hardly fault Jill for not working to support herself: the Updike male does not ask that of his women. But it is rather a fear of new qualities in Jill, nonexistent in his other women, that disturbs Harry. She knows a world of drugs, freedom, and ideas, all incomprehensible to him. Because she makes love with any man who wants her, he assumes she can have no feeling for him. Like his other lovers, she desires and needs him, but she is so unlike them that he does not admit to her kind of need. Only his son Nelson is aware of it. Nelson's camaraderie with Jill is another thing that threatens Harry. These young people are more mature than he is and make a conscious attempt to educate themselves, a process quite foreign to Harry. He is on sure ground as he watches young boys play basketball, but he has no sense of these new mental games. He is thus hostile to this new kind of woman who suggests them, "wombing" Jill, as she says, as if to violate her hardness.

Jill pleads with Harry to protect her from the drugs Skeeter attempts to force upon her. Even though she may consider Harry old-fashioned, only he can save her from the doom of her own time, in particular the addiction she has suffered from before. There is something to rely on in Harry which Janice also appreciates over the years as she watches him work at a tedious job to support her and Nelson. In growing older Harry has hardened into an unpleasant conservatism, but it is this kind of a bias that strengthens his loyalty to his father and his responsibility for his wife and child. This common man cannot match the dramatic sense of Skeeter's diabolism, but he does, with some honor, what a man

can do in a bizarre world of moon landings, drugs, and a Vietnam war: he
provides for his family and stays with them (until Janice leaves him). Jill, however, is too new and strange to be included in Harry's loyalties. She realizes after
futile trying that she can never be anything in his "real life."

When Jill first becomes a part of Harry's household she is distinguished as
a superior woman by being a good cook, her "filet of sole, lemony, light, sim-
mered in sunshine." With mock pastoral lyricism Updike evokes an aura around
such items as the coffee she brews, which is "black nectar compared to the
watery tar Janice used to serve." But even Jill's excellent cookery fails as Harry's
coolness toward her intensifies: the girl who is thin and hard and sexless now
serves rubbery lamb chops and charred chicken livers with frozen insides (an
unfortunately prophetic image for her).

However else he might consider her, Harry can never say that Jill is stupid.
Her intellectuality may not be deep, but she does think and make an attempt to
be educated, something new to the Updike heroine. Seeing the low educational
level of the Angstrom household, she decides to cultivate Nelson. Harry is invited
to join Jill and her eager pupil in lengthy discussions of God, beauty, and religion. Harry never complains of these learning sessions, but they are strange and
threatening to him. On one occasion he loses an erection with Jill when "all her
talk, her wild wanting it, have scared him down to nothing."

Since Harry considers a woman only in terms of her sexuality, he suspects
that Jill must be Nelson's instructor in sex (with no real basis for this assumption). His resentment of her makes him fascinated with Skeeter's schemes to
destroy her. At this point something sinister occurs in Updike's writing: he
allows his bias in behalf of the stupid-sexual woman to intrude to the point of
forcing a violent death (and violence is not usually his subject) upon this intelligent girl whom he dislikes and cannot deal with. In creating a new type of
woman and brutally disposing of her Updike seems unaware of what he does,
not only in terms of artistic distortion but as a revelation of his determination to
preserve a bovine image of women. In doing so, his character Harry, in regard to
Jill, must become callous to the point of a cruelty that is not in character for
him, even in his most destructive acts. He is so taken by Skeeter's rituals that he
joins with him in abusing Jill. At Skeeter's request Harry reads from *The Life
and Times of Frederick Douglass* the section about Esther, a beautiful slave girl
who is whipped by a master who is " 'cruelly deliberate, and protracted the
torture as one who was delighted with the agony of his victim.' " After the
reading Skeeter grabs Jill by the throat and rips her white (mock-virginal) dress
while Harry watches, his instinct "not to rescue her but to shield Nelson," who
moans that she will be killed. Harry disagrees, suggesting that anyway she probably likes what Skeeter does to her.

Either Harry imagines that women love to suffer, or he is glad to see this particular girl suffer, which is more likely the case. Charles Thomas Samuels perceptively questions why Harry would watch the humiliation of the white woman so willingly. He suggests that perhaps Harry hates Jill for being upper-class with the same intensity that Skeeter resents whites. Samuels is quite right in questioning the motivation for Harry's odd behavior, which even Skeeter cannot understand. But there is little in either of the Rabbit novels to indicate such an intense concern with the upper class. The real preoccupation is with being a successful lover. Thus Jill, who talks too much and thinks too much, is a failure as a lover, and it is this which Harry truly resents, not her wealth.

Harry's characteristic passivity is partially responsible for his failure to help Jill. He is passive regarding Janice's love affair, the loss of his job, and his son's antagonism toward him. But there is a difference in his failure to act in regard to Jill which reflects a genuine satisfaction with her misfortune. What should be a truly frightening event—his house burning with Jill inside—is a serene occasion. We would not necessarily expect Harry to dash into the flames to save Jill. But his placidity shows something newly disturbing about him. There is no horror as she burns to death (and we know how capable he is of panic) in what is a rare scene of violence for Updike. As Jill dies, Harry talks quietly to his son, not as a man stunned or sickened, but as an extraordinarily callous person who would stand by and let a fellow being die. Nelson reflects the terror his father should feel, and after accusing him of letting Jill die, he runs into the burning house to save her himself. He knows she must be inside, as we all do, but Harry says vaguely, " 'She must have gotten out. . . . She's safe and far away.' "

If shock were the reason for Harry's calm, then we might expect him to be horrified later on when he realizes the manner in which Jill has died. But his sorrow for the loss of his wife, his job, and his home includes hardly a notice of Jill. The question of whether he might have saved her aside, there is no *feeling* for her death. Harry makes a peculiar analogy of his part in Jill's death with Janice's accidental killing of their daughter June: "Her trip drowns babies; his burns girls." If he considers himself guilty, then he also considers Janice guilty of June's death. But if he sees the baby's death simply as a terrible accident, which he is by now inclined to do, then by his analogy he takes no responsibility for letting Jill die. But the cases are not the same. One significant difference between the two incidents is the impact on the persons involved: for Janice, the baby's death is a tragedy of the first order, both because her child dies and because she causes the accident. She will suffer a lifetime for it. On the other hand, Harry is hardly affected by Jill's death, which he might have prevented. It is no accident that he so calmly watches the house burn with her inside.

The construction of *Rabbit Redux* is deeply flawed in that Updike uses unlike incidents, June's death and Jill's death, to provide an apparent symmetry of plot as a way of balancing out the Angstrom marriage. But what is far more disturbing is that Updike allows his bias in favor of stupid women to determine that a thinking woman must be killed off. Jill is also one of the few women in Updike who falls outside the sacred category of wife, and in this world of couples, extra women must be disposed of one way or another. In *Rabbit Redux* Janice is restored to her marriage; Ruth is now married with children, the wife she was always considered to be; Jill is dead, hauled away in a rubber bag; and Rabbit's sister Mim, a visitor from the West Coast, which might for its foreignness be the Ivory Coast, is only allowed to pass through town.

Mim was always the exotic member of the Angstrom family, adding a barbaric note even in high school when she wore earrings that made her look like a gypsy or an Arab. She arrives from California as if from another planet, her life jangling to a foreign tune, "her eyes, which are inhuman, Egyptian, drenched in peacock purple and blue." Mim is Updike's career girl, with the only career he can imagine for a woman, prostitution. Mim knows things. She understands about Rabbit and Janice and others in Mt. Judge and helpfully goes to bed with Charlie Stavros to precipitate Janice's return to her husband. Harry is affectionate with his sister, an affection which in Updike's frame of reference can only be demonstrated by the male's erotic attraction to the female. As Harry embraces Mim he wants to feel all the men who have already held her.

But there is something hopeless about Mim which puts her beyond the pale of society, related, no doubt, to her type of prostitution (like Jill's cold promiscuity), a tougher version than Ruth's vulnerable whoring and one entailing an involvement in worldly experience which in Updike's society is not acceptable for a woman. When she becomes in any way competent and self-supportive, a woman must be dehumanized. (Obviously the issue is not merely prostitution, because Updike approves of certain kinds of prostitutes.) Mim says people in California build hard shells around themselves, almost as the sun bakes them brown; she is paid for what she gives, "because anything free has a rattlesnake under it." As he does with the creation of Jill, Updike equates Mim's intelligence with the absence of the sexuality which makes a woman desirable as a wife and a bona fide member of society. A woman cannot be both intelligent and sexually desirable; thus Mim is dehumanized, to an even greater extent than are the sexual automatons of Tarbox, who are at least wives. Her smile and laugh appear as "electronic images" created by a coded tape fed into her head. Her only purpose for existence is to be used by men with failed careers and broken marriages, who, like her, are merely waste products of society.

Only a few other single girls drift through Updike's stories, one an odd-looking and pitiful girl of twenty-nine, Penelope Vogel of "Eros Rampant," whom Richard Maple believes only a Negro could make love to now. (Maple never makes clear the nature of his own involvement with Penelope, which we can only surmise to be sexual, given Updike's outlook on men's singular attraction to women.) If she is sexual enough, the single girl, such as Rebecca Cune in "Snowing in Greenwich Village" (Cune equals cunt, according to the Hamiltons' study), is a natural threat to other marriages, as are all divorcées, the few of them that exist. Divorce appears to change the nature of the wife automatically from her good-natured open desirability into a mean, threatening quality. While one's undesirable traits may surface with the strain of divorce, such a condition is highly exaggerated by Updike, who shows that someone like Angela Hanema becomes immediately and thoroughly distasteful when she divorces. She is now a threatening being who will not be allowed to remain in her separate condition. Like the single woman (always a version of prostitute), she must become a wife or be disposed of.

The new, more strident and independent woman is clearly a threat to the Updike male. Such an attitude is explicit in the story "Marching through Boston," written with a humor that not often enough surfaces in Updike's fiction. The problem of the male ego is faced directly as a wife takes up an interest in life outside the home. The Maples are now entering middle age, after love affairs for both, contemplated divorce, and a transfusion to liven their marriage ("Giving Blood"). Joan Maple's burgeoning interest in the civil rights movement suggests a genuine concern which was never true, for example, when Janice Angstrom took her part-time job. But in both cases the venture outside the home is a threat to the marriage.

Joan Maple, in glowing health, her voice melodious as she makes her business calls (her husband even thinks her posture has improved), is having the fun of doing something well. Richard Maple is pointed out as the husband of the woman who makes such good speeches. She persuades him to march with her in Boston, which as we would expect turns out to be as miserable an experience for him as it is an exhilarating one for her. His whole body resists the intrusion of his wife's outside life, and he starts the day with a fever (a man who has weathered her love affairs in good health). After the march he goes to his sickbed, raving at the foolishness of the speeches, while Joan, who cannot soothe him, gaily makes calls from the downstairs phone. This story explicitly announces that signs of intelligence, independence, or strength in a woman are considered threatening to a man. But while Updike is aware of such an attitude in this case, which he treats lightly, he seems oblivious to its pernicious effects in *Rabbit Redux*.

In the story "Home" a young father returning to America after living in London sees his mother waiting on the dock with the "face of a woman whose country has never quite settled what to do with its women." Updike has expressed a concern with correcting this problem as it occurs in our literature: "American fiction is notoriously thin on women, and I *have* attempted a number of portraits of women, and we may have reached that point of civilization, or decadence, where we can look at women." The "we" for Updike, which can mean only the male point of view, betrays the impossibility of his being able to look at a broad spectrum of women or to deal in much detail with their feelings. But the fact that he so seldom attempts to show the woman's point of view does not necessarily negate his portraits of those women who have allowed themselves to be formed by the concepts of men.

As a progression from the manipulating mothers of the past, Updike accepts only the bovine wives who comfortably merge with his failing heroes. It is here that he apparently wishes the development of women to end. The current wave of feminism is very much related to the stagnant conditions he portrays, but Updike offers a backlash effect as he denigrates new kinds of women. Under the guise of tolerant acceptance, his fiction insidiously goes about making female mediocrity and inertia seem inevitable, even lovable. And he consistently reasserts the worn dichotomy that a woman is sexual and stupid (human) or that she is frigid and intelligent (inhuman). Only the woman as a comfortable blank is to be desired and accepted by individual men and by society. Women who do not fit this standard are not really human and must be rubbed out of the world.

JAMES M. MELLARD

The Novel as Lyric Elegy:
The Mode of Updike's The Centaur

Several critics have alluded to what is a most crucial matter in John Updike's
The Centaur, the location of point of view in the novel, but it remained for
Edward P. Vargo, a decade after *The Centaur*'s publication, to put the issue
bluntly: "the entire novel is presented to us as the experience of Peter, reliving
three days in his life with his father, while he lies beside his black mistress in
varying states of wakefulness or sleep . . . The entire novel is a fusion of the
dreams and reveries and actual narration of Peter." While I agree with the con-
tention that Peter is the origin of the narration, I must disagree with Vargo's
further argument that "the experience takes on the character of a rite for Peter."
For Vargo to call the novel a "rite" or "ritual" not only contradicts the language
of his second statement above, it also suggests that Peter plays a more public and
ceremonial, even priestly, role than he does. The central issue may be nothing
but a problem of definition. I suspect it is much more, however — being instead
one of *modal* perception. In literary analysis, ritual is more properly associated
with drama or the dramatic mode in fiction, but *The Centaur* is neither one nor
the other. Rather, its art is essentially lyrical, the expressive symbol of Peter's
elegiac feelings for his father. Peter's relation to the novel, therefore, is primarily
that of the lyric poet to the poem in which every detail ultimately comes out of
the creative center of the poet's emotions.

I

Peter Caldwell gives the novel its lyrical, elegiac shape. It is he who
accounts for the novel's point of view, its shifting formal modes, and, above all,

From *Texas Studies in Literature and Language* 21, no. 1 (Spring 1979). © 1979 by the
University of Texas Press.

for its metamorphic verbal styles. The role he plays as narrator is much like that of Hart Crane's poetic persona in *The Bridge*, embedded in the second section of the poem, the one entitled "The Harbor Dawn" in "Powhatan's Daughter." As in Crane's long poem, Updike's narrator does not appear as a narrative persona until a portion of the story has been presented. In *The Bridge* one first sees both the "Proem" and "Ave Maria"; in *The Centaur* one sees the long chapter devoted to Caldwell-Chiron's receiving his arrow wound, visiting Hummel-Hephaestus to have it removed, and later resuming his classroom duties. When Peter does appear in his role as narrator it is precisely in the situation of Crane's persona, who is lying abed with his lover-mistress:

> And you beside me, blessed now while sirens
> Sing to us, stealthily weave us into day —
> Serenely now, before day claims our eyes
> Your cool arms murmurously about me lay.
>
> (*The Bridge*)

Peter enters *The Centaur* having just "dreamed," as he sleeps beside his lover, the account of a day in the life of his father given in chapter 1: "I wake now," he tells us, "often to silence, beside you, with a pang of fear, after dreams that leave a sour wash of atheism in my stomach . . . But in those days I always awoke to the sound of my parents talking, voices which even in agreement were contentious and full of life."

Recurrently throughout the novel, Peter and his lover appear in the apparent relationship of storyteller to audience. In chapter 4 Peter asks, "Why is it, love, that faces we love look upon each remeeting so fresh, as if our hearts have in this instant again minted them?" In chapter 8 he says, "My love, listen. Or are you asleep? It doesn't matter." Shortly after this, he says, "my story is coming to its close," and, just a little later, he also says, "The weariness I felt [after spending the night at the home of the Hummels] overtakes me in the telling." But these brief notations identify Peter not so much in the role of a story *teller* as in the role of a lyric *persona* from whose experiences and emotions the novel grows. His role as mythic "poet," analogous, perhaps, to his vocation as an abstract expressionist painter, may give Peter an audience, but it is not an audience for which a "rite" could be performed such as Vargo perceives. As Peter realizes, an "external" audience "doesn't matter," for the lyrical expression, whatever form it takes, is mainly personal and private. The poet is his own audience.

The lyrical persona in fiction and poetry, often playing a metamorphic role, assumes many guises, many poses, many voices. In his role as a lyrical persona, Peter thus accounts for what [Arthur] Mizener calls the "mixture of genres," the different "modes of narration" in *The Centaur*. But rather than "nominal and ineffective," as Mizener claims, Peter's role as lyrical persona simply exists *in* the various modes and voices and is effective in direct proportion to the extent to which Peter's own voice is disguised. The lyric poet's effectiveness comes in the achieved virtuosity of the poem. If a Crane can "speak," as L. S. Dembo says, through dream, meditation, and ecstasy in *The Bridge*, or a William Carlos Williams can "speak" through meditation, narrative, newspaper extracts, geological tables, and virtually every other form of human expression in *Paterson*, surely Updike's Peter Caldwell can speak through the objective omniscience of chapter 1, the first person of chapters 2, 4, and 8, the formally decorous pastoral myth of chapters 3 and 9, the newspaper obituary of chapter 5, the first-person stream of consciousness of chapter 6, and the alternating third-person objectivity of chapter 7. In *The Centaur*, as in the long yet essentially lyric poem (such as *The Waste Land*, *The Bridge*, and *Paterson*), the main principle of narrative is change, variation, discontinuity. But as there is always at the center of such poems a single figure (Tiresias, Crane, Noah F. Paterson) through whom the poet projects his voices, poses, guises, so at the center of *The Centaur* is the figure of Peter Caldwell.

The metamorphic and metamorphosing role of the persona in lyrical art also has considerable importance in other ways. Of primary significance in *The Centaur* is the way in which this persona determines the shape-shifting style. Speaking to his love about his life with his family, Peter says in one place, "We moved, somehow, on a firm stage, resonant with metaphor." Peter's expressive, dreamlike, imaginative recreation of that world is itself "resonant with metaphor," and much of the texture of narrative comes from the metaphorical habit of language Updike gives Peter's narrative voices. The world of metaphor takes over entirely in those chapters, such as 1, 3, 6, and 9, in which Caldwell is Chiron and, as in 6, when Peter is Prometheus; in these chapters there is no projected distance between the figures in the narrative and the metaphorical world of myth. Yet even here the multiple perspectives of the novel's style permit the irony and humor of something very like the lowly pun. *Inside* this world the characters don't know that they are not simply "people," but are centaurs and gods and the like living in what, from *our* perspective, is a *locus amoenus*. Thus, on a single page the centaur can say to Hummel-Hephaestus, "I got to *high-tail* it." And when the mechanic will not take any money for having removed the arrow from the centaur's ankle, George can think, "And this was the way with all these Olinger aristocrats. They wouldn't take any money but they did take an authoritative tone. They forced a favor on you and *that made them gods*." Finally, when Hummel tells George the days are bad, George can reply, "It's no *Golden Age*, that's for sure." These words — "high-tail," "gods," "Golden Age" — become virtual puns, but only to us and to the one who dreams the dream.

Because we share Peter's multiple perspective, we are the ones who have the binocular ability to encompass the mythic past and the nonmythic present. Such a vision is required to see the play on words.

But Peter's expression neither moves always in that world of total metaphor, which is one pole of the dialectic of language, nor in the world of total realism, the other pole of language, identified by Peter as that "patch of Pennsylvania in 1947," the world emphasized by those critics like Mizener who value Updike's realism. There is, besides, a middle ground discernible in Peter's style. When the projected distance between the mythic and the realistic worlds increases, Peter's verbal technique shifts to the simile. As Peter uses them, the similes make connections between the other two polar realms by using "like" and "as" and "seems." When, for instance, George Caldwell speaks of Peter's skin condition to the hitchhiker, Peter, who is also rock-bound Prometheus, reports to us: "*In effect* my father had torn off my clothes and displayed my prickling scabs. In the glare of my anger his profile *seemed* that of a *blind raw rock*." Similarly, Peter narrates about the hitchhiker, who is Hermes (or the winged Mercury): "through the dusty rear window I watched our guest, looking *like a messenger* with his undisclosed bundle, dwindle. The hitchhiker became a brown wisp at the mouth of the bridge, *flew upwards, vanished*." Such simile—but with an occasional ascent into metaphor—plays a very large part in Peter's style when he relates details about himself. Of his skin problem, for example, he says: "Had the world been watching, it would have been startled, for my belly, *as if pecked by a great bird*, was dotted with red scabs the size of coins." Of his bright red shirt (behind which stands the image of Prometheus's gift of fire to man), Peter remarks: "I would carry to my classmates on this bitter day a *gift of scarlet, a giant spark*, a two-pocketed emblem of heat." In other places, both as first and third persons, he speaks similarly about that shirt: "I unbuttoned my pea jacket so the devil-may-care *flame* of my shirt showed"; "My shirt was eating my skin with *fire*"; "*On fire* . . . , he turns his red back on the crowd."

Peter also speaks of other characters in terms of simile. Doc Appleton's mythic identity is Apollo, so Peter uses similes to draw into the texture of narrative two of Apollo's main roles, as the sun who brings light and as the slayer of the serpent, Python, at Delphi. When Doc Appleton (Apollo was also a healer) speaks his name, Peter says, "*like a ray of sunlight* the old man's kindness and competence pierced the morbid atmosphere of his house." And when the doctor puts down his stethoscope, Peter says, "it *writhed* and then subsided *like a slain rubber serpent*." Minor Kretz, who runs the luncheonette where all the school kids hang out, is offered as a parallel to Minos, King of Crete, whose erotic interest is Pasiphae (Mrs. Passify in the novel). Of the man who runs the luncheonette and the woman who runs the post office next door, Peter says, "the symmetry [between the two establishments], carried right down to the worn spots of the two floors and the heating pipes running along the opposing walls, was so perfect that as a child I had imagined that Mrs. Passify and Minor Kretz were secretly married." But Minor is also the minotaur (*borne* by Queen Pasiphae), so at one point Peter speaks of Minor's place as "a maze"; he says also, "Minor *charged* over to our booth. Anger flashed from his bald dome and *steamed* through his *flared nostrils*. 'Here, hyaar,' he *snorted*"; and later he says, "The luncheonette . . . is all but empty, like a stage . . . Within, Minor is a cauldron of rage; his *hairy nostrils seem seething vents*." Zimmerman, the school principal, doubles, in the mythic world, as Zeus. The narrator or the other characters thus refer to him several times in figures that suggest his role as an Olympian god. George Caldwell, for example, moans, "I could feel Zimmerman sitting in there *like a big heavy raincloud*"; and later the narrator says, "Zimmerman sees *as if through a rift in clouds* that Caldwell's glimpse of Mrs. Herzog is at the bottom of his fear and his mind exults." At another time Peter thinks of Zimmerman's finger (like that of Michelangelo's God) as "dense with existence."

Finally, Peter's father also comes in for figurative treatment in those chapters where realism dominates myth. The main referent for Peter's images, of course, is the equine portion of the mythic centaur's body. Thus, for example, once when Peter and his father are walking together, we are told: "We seemed from our shadow to be a prancing one-headed creature with four legs." At another time, when George has felt Zimmerman as "a dark cloud" around him, we read: "*Lifting his head and sniffing*, Caldwell experiences a vivid urge to walk on faster, *to canter* right past Hummel's, *to romp neighing* through the front door and out the back door of any house in Olinger that stood in his way, *to gallop* up the brushy winter-burned flank of Shale Hill and on, on, over hills that grow smoother and bluer with distance, on and on." And near the end of the novel, Peter sees his father walking toward home: "His shape before me was made less human by the bag of groceries he was carrying and it seemed, my legs having ceased to convey the sensations of walking, that *his was the shape of the neck and head of a horse I was riding*."

Figurative language such as this suggests one extra dimension Updike gives *The Centaur*. There is a very real sense in which Peter's search through his memory and imagination, in the process of "dreaming" this narrative, is for an original, innocent, prelapsarian world "resonant with metaphor." He searches for a world in which identities exist between reality and myth, existence and dream, earth and heaven, but the very *need* to speak of Appleton, Minor Kretz, or his father in terms of simile—of "as," "like," "seems"—reveals the distance the youth has fallen away, has descended from his golden age. Consequently,

Updike's epigraph for the book, from Karl Barth, creates an appropriate context for the uses Peter makes of language, for Peter is that creature Barth describes, "the creature on the boundary between heaven and earth," between the "creation inconceivable to man" and the "creation conceivable to him." The novel thus represents Peter's effort to recapture through the lyricist's powers of language an image made resonant by his father of the most felicitous time in his life.

II

As a result of Peter's role in it and the attitude he brings, *The Centaur* belongs to that genre of lyrical expressions known as the elegiac. Larry E. Taylor has detailed many of the formal ways in which Updike has created a pastoral elegy. To begin with, Taylor suggests that the four interspersed short chapters — chapters 3, 5, 8, 9 — help to generate the pastoral elegiac structure because each is a variation of a basic convention of the traditional form, both in its subject matter and in its language and imagery. "The language of these touchstone chapters," Taylor writes, "provides the lyricism and formality required to keep the novel from being ironic, satiric, and comic. Seen as a highly personal expression of both Updike's and Peter's sense of loss (Updike has left Shillington to become a writer for the *New Yorker*, and Peter is painting abstractions in a New York loft), *The Centaur* appeals to the impersonality of stock pastoral conventions as a vehicle for transforming life into art — the personal into the universal." Drawing upon elements achieved by Milton in the *spirit* of the pastoral in an elegy such as *Lycidas*, Taylor outlines the parallels between the novel and the poem in subject matter. But the limitations Taylor sets for himself will not allow him to get into the detailed analysis of those narrative and thematic patterns in the novel that relate directly to the more conventional elegiac elements. The most important such patterns are those associated with the elegy's concern with matters of eschatology, the "furthest things" — time, death, man's goal, or end, or *telos*.

One of the major concerns in *The Centaur* is with time. It is manifest in Peter's interest in the knowable historical past and the unknowable future. To know the past, Peter believes, is to know more about the present, so he is always fascinated by details of the lives of people he knows, whether the details concern the more intimate relationships of a woman like Vera Hummel to various men or just the public triumph of one like Zimmerman on the Olinger track team. But even more than the past or the present Peter is concerned with and believes in the future. It is in the future that he believes his desires can be fulfilled. He knows, for example, that in the normal course of things, he will outlive Zimmerman, his father's viciously petty supervisor, so the future holds his dream: "Triumphantly,

Peter feels descend upon him, his father's avenger, this advantage over the antagonist: he has more years to live. Ignorant and impotent here and now, in the
dimension of the future he is mighty." For Peter the future becomes his dimension, its airy spaces his natural element, as water is Deifendorf's: "The world of
water was closed to me," he thinks, "so I had fallen in love with the air, which I
was able to seize in great thrilling condensations within me that I labeled the
Future: it was in this realm that I hoped to reward my father for his suffering."

What, no doubt, Peter wishes to reward his father with is a reply to the
question his father asks: it is a simple, but ultimate, question, "what's the answer?" Once he has inhabited his imagined future, however, Peter must admit
that he is as impotent there as he was in the past to find "the answer." Neither
his chosen form of artistic expression nor erotic attachment has given him answers to his eschatological questions. *Inside* his future he says:

> I glance around at the nest we have made, at the floorboards polished
> by our bare feet, at the *continents* of stain on the ceiling like an
> old and all-wrong *discoverer's map*, at the earnestly bloated can-
> vases I conscientiously cover with great streaks *straining to say what
> even I am beginning to suspect is the unsayable thing*, and I grow
> frightened. I consider the life we have made together, with its days
> spent without relation to the days the sun keeps and its baroque
> arabesques of increasingly attenuated emotion and its furnishings
> like a scattering of worn-out Braques and its rather wistful half-
> Freudian half-Oriental sex-mysticism, and I wonder, *Was it for this
> that my father gave up his life?*

There are no empirical truths in eschatology, and while abstract expressionism
and erotic mysticism may allow one to pursue his own personal answers, they
will permit one only to say the thing to oneself, not to say the unsayable to
another. The truths Peter may discover empirically and may relate concretely,
rather than abstractly, lie in his experience. Experience itself can lead him to an
appropriate art and a transcendent love, and the center of that experience is his
relationship to his father.

Death is the furthest thing in man's experience, for it is the last final thing
empirically he knows will happen to him. As most readers of *The Centaur*
know, death is the primary concern of the novel, as it is the primary concern of
most of Updike's work. The general theme is itself teleological, involving as it
does man's end, his place in the universal scheme of things. This particular
aspect of the eschatological, elegiac theme is exhaustively presented in the various
cosmological systems the novel invokes. These systems are really "myths" of one
sort or another. They appear in two groups, one broadly "scientific," the other

broadly "humanistic." Among the scientific are the "myth" of biological evolution, the myths suggested by modern cosmological astronomy, and the mythic narrative of the oxygen cycle in nature; among the humanistic are the pastoral myths of the Greeks and the Christians. Each of these myths represents an attempt by man to explain and/or to come to terms with the question of his own predestined end. In the elegiac *form* of the narrative we can see Peter review and discard the various "answers" until he discovers his own adequate answer in his myth of Art.

A *mythos* is a traditional story, and it is as a traditional *story* that George Caldwell tells to his class the history of biological evolution. He does it in terms of the "creation-clock" all of us have seen in one place or another. He begins with the estimated age of the universe, five billion years, speaks of various stars —the sun, Venus, Alpha Centauri, the Milky Way, the constellation Sagittarius —and of the hundred billion galaxies, each containing a hundred billion stars, numbers, in their unfathomableness, that remind Caldwell of death. Consequently, he says to his class, "Let's try to reduce five billion years to our size. Let's say the universe is three days old. Today is Thursday . . . Last Monday at noon there was the greatest explosion there ever was. We're still riding on it." This explosion, he tells his class, came five billion years ago from a "primeval egg," one cubic centimeter of which weighed two hundred and fifty tons. After a period of darkness and "the expanding flux of universal substance," stars begin to shine, the Earth begins to form, and "for a whole day . . . , between Tuesday and Wednesday noon, the earth is barren. There is no life on it. Just ugly rocks, stale water, vomiting volcanoes, everything slithering and sliding and maybe freezing now and then as the sun like a dirty old light bulb flickered up there in the sky. By yesterday noon, a little life showed up. Nothing spectacular; just a little bit of slime. All yesterday afternoon, and most of the night, life remained microscopic." With the advent of microscopic life, the evolutionary process accelerates rapidly. But Caldwell's concern, like every man's, lies in the relation of life to death. Thus, "the volvox, of these early citizens in the kingdom of life, interests us because he invented death . . . by pioneering this new idea of *co-operation*, [the volvox] rolled life into the kingdom of certain—as opposed to accidental—death . . . It dies sacrificially, for the good of the whole, . . . the first altruists. The first do-gooders. If I had a hat on, I'd take it off to 'em." The story of life goes very quickly now, from trilobites to the first vertebrate fishes, the first plants, the insects, the reptiles, and the mammals. Finally, at a point when Caldwell's "very blood loathed the story he had told, 'One minute ago, flint-chipping, fire-kindling, death-foreseeing, a tragic animal appeared . . . called Man.'"

In this now traditional story, man knows he is at the apex of a process that explains the fact of death. But knowledge cannot reconcile this tragic animal to the death he foresees. Neither can the "humanistic values implicit in the physical sciences" Zimmerman speaks of in his report on Caldwell's lecture on the *mythos* of biological evolution. Caldwell's thought upon seeing the phrase is, "Maybe down deep in the atom there's a little man sitting in a rocking chair reading the evening paper." Nor can the *mythos* of astronomy, the theory of the "big-bang" according to Hoyle. We discover astronomy's limitations when Peter imagines a universe falling through space as he watches snowflakes falling beneath a tall light:

> Directly under the light, the wavering fall of the particles is projected as an erratic oscillation, but away from the center, where the light rays strike obliquely, the projection parabolically magnifies the speed of the shadow as it hastens forward to meet its flake. The shadows stream out of infinity, slow, and, each darkly sharp in its last instant, vanish as their originals kiss the white plane . . . He turns scientist and dispassionately tries to locate in the cosmography his father has taught him an analogy between the phenomenon he has observed and the "red shift" whereby the stars appear to be retreating at a speed proportional to their distance from us. Perhaps this is a kindred illusion, perhaps—he struggles to picture it—the stars are in fact falling gently through a cone of observation of which our earthly telescopes are the apex.

Peter can find a place from which to observe the relative motions of this snow-flake galaxy, but that place in his imagined universe, "pinned, stretched, crucified like a butterfly upon a frame of unvarying geometrical truth," gives him little security. Walking away from the light he seems "to arrive at a kind of edge where the speed of the shadows is infinite and a small universe both ends and does not end." Thus the vision he has here of the universe as it is pictured by modern astronomy gives Peter little consolation. Only by returning his gaze to the concrete reality of the town can Peter overcome what he thinks of as the "sickly" nature of his "cosmic thoughts."

The *mythos* of astronomy suggests to Peter a one-way process, of man and man's life disappearing into a nebulous "center," a cosmic black hole such as those only recently discovered by astronomers. Consequently, the *mythos* of the oxygen cycle as it is seen in the formula

$$C_6 H_{12} O_6 + 6O_2 = 6CO_2 + 6H_2 O + E$$

may be somewhat more appeasing to one's imagination. The formula represents the creation of energy and, thus, of life. As Caldwell explains to his class,

" 'When this process stops'—he Xed through the equation—'*this* stops'—he double-Xed out the E—'and you become what they call dead. You become a worthless log of old chemicals.' " But at least this process can be reversed. The equation can also be read backwards in order to represent the process of photosynthesis that occurs in plants: "that's the way the world goes round . . . Round and round, and where it stops, nobody knows." The formula thus offers man an objective symbol for the *cyclic* process of death and renewal in nature. It *may* offer the illusion of death and renewal for man himself.

The *mythoi* of the Greeks and the Christians suggest man as an individual can achieve the immortality once foresaken by that altruistic volvox. Moreover, these myths are more personal than the symbols for the organic process. They return human consciousness to the equations that science has formulated, and, at least potentially, they can express and contain the emotional impact of death. But for Peter, the Greek myths seem more germane than the Christian. Many critics read the novel as if it were a paean to the traditional church, yet Christianity in *The Centaur* offers little more than those myths of science. There really is not much to cling to in the doctrines expressed by its representative, the Reverend March. George comes to him troubled in mind and seeking "the answer" he has sought from others. "I can't make it add up," he says to March, "and I'd be grateful for your viewpoint." George's own view, for example, of the difference between Lutherans and Calvinists is, "the Lutherans say Jesus Christ is the only answer and the Calvinists say whatever happens to you, happens to you, is the answer." The son of a minister, George also has a certain conception of Presbyterian doctrine: "there are the elect and the non-elect, the ones that have it and the ones that don't, and the ones that don't have it are never going to get it. What I could never ram through my thick skull was why the ones that don't have it were created in the first place." March's reply to these ideas is ministerial jargon about orthodoxy, Christocentrism, substantive Eucharistic transformation, and understanding the doctrine of predestination "as counterbalanced by the doctrine of God's infinite mercy."

None of the Reverend March's answers is concrete enough for George to grasp. To George God's mercy itself is one of the furthest things, for it is "infinite at an infinite distance" from man as he lives his life. There is nothing either in the substance or the tone of what the Reverend says that will reconcile George to the death he lately has come to face. And there is nothing any more affirmative in the Christian cosmology the novel offers elsewhere, in a passage occurring just before the dialogue between Caldwell and the Reverend. The same snowstorm that gives Peter his cosmic thoughts enters into Updike's elaborate metaphor of Olinger as "yet one more Bethlehem. Behind a glowing window the infant God squalls. Out of zero all has come to birth. The panes, tinted by the straw of the crib within, hush its cries. The world goes on unhearing. The town of white roofs seems a colony of deserted temples; they feather together with distance and go gray, melt." Whether it is only because the town does not listen or whether the infant is just one more rough beast, shuffling toward Bethlehem, such a vision can offer no consolation to one who has the thoughts besetting George Caldwell. Since they can not reconcile George, neither can they offer reconciliation to Peter Caldwell.

The Greek myths one sees in those interchapters offer much more to *The Centaur*. Their substance can be no more meaningful than the *mythoi* of evolution, astronomy, the oxygen cycle, or even Christianity. But the affective significance they bring to the novel gives them priority over all those others, for it is finally the emotional response to the fact of death that Peter's lyrical expression must contain. The Greek myths, more than the other *mythoi*, seem to express the archetypes that create the concrete patterns Updike favors and that Peter must eventually accept in his vision of Art. Carl Jung says that primitive man does not create his myths, he *experiences* them. In *The Centaur* it is the experiencing of Greek myth that we see, for these chapters (3, 9) more than any others are ones in which the world "resonant with metaphor" is achieved. Because Chiron *is* the centaur in these chapters, there is no distance between the mythic world man desires and the real world in which he resides. Consequently, when Chiron speaks to his students on "the Genesis of all things," there seems little in the story to make his blood sicken as Caldwell's does when he relates the *mythos* of evolution: "In the beginning," he says, "blackwinged Night was courted by the wind, and laid a silver egg in the womb of Darkness. From this egg hatched Eros . . . And Love set the Universe in motion . . . Men lived without cares or labor . . . Death, to them, was no more terrible than sleep."

Such a story, idyllic in both content and tone, can offer to Peter not only a symbolic narrative archetype that expresses in human terms the meaning of the oxygen cycle; it also offers a symbol to contain his feelings of love and goodwill toward his father. This archetype is connected to the themes of the pastoral elegy, but it also relates directly to the role of the scapegoat-dying god George Caldwell plays. It thus balances the wasteland against Arcadia, and in the formal pattern of the elegy, it joins Nature and human nature. Both father and son participate in the pattern because of their identifications with Nature itself. Each is related to the seasonal rhythm in some way: Peter's psoriasis, for instance, is a "rhythmic curse that breathed in and out with [God's] seasons"; George's whole life— identified as it is with his birthdate near the winter solstice (just before Christmas)—and his role as the constellation Sagittarius seems interconnected with natural patterns. George himself, in relation to his son, becomes not just the "old man" Peter must replace or "trade in for"; he becomes "Old Man Winter's belly," that archetypal figure of the wasteland who holds life in bondage. But even as the Old Man or as Winter's belly, George can offer Peter hope. Although the "emasculate" Sky might leave "his progeny to parch upon a white waste," George can think: "Yet even in the dead of winter the sere twigs prepare their small dull buds. In the pit of the year a king was born. Not a leaf falls but leaves an amber root, a dainty hoof, a fleck of baggage to be unpacked in future time." The hope George can leave Peter is finally to be found in Nature itself.

III

The Greek myths allow Peter to discover the one *mythos* which is appropriate for him. That is *art* as an eschatology, as a way of expressing and containing those furthest things that trouble man. Peter's grandfather Caldwell had religion, his father had science, and Peter—the end of the classic decline from priest, to teacher, to artist—has Art. To Peter, Art, "however clumsy and quaint and mistaken," can radiate "the innocence and hope, the hope of seizing something and holding it fast, that enters whenever a brush touches canvas." The paintings of Vermeer provide him with manifestations of that hope. They become, he says, "the Holy Ghost" of his adolescence: "that these paintings, which I had worshipped in reproduction, had a simple physical existence seemed a profound mystery to me: to come within touching distance of their surfaces, to see with my own eyes the truth of their color, the tracery of the cracks whereby time had inserted itself like a mystery within a mystery, would have been for me to enter a Real Presence so ultimate I would not be surprised to die in the encounter." It becomes Peter's dream to be able to create in the profound way of a Vermeer. Eventually, Peter has a revelation as to how he too can create art's mystery within a mystery. He says, "I must go to Nature disarmed of perspective and stretch myself like a large transparent canvas upon her in the hope that, my submission being perfect, the imprint of a beautiful and useful truth would be taken." It is a recognition that bears out Vargo's explanation of the connection of Updike's novel to Karl Barth's philosophy: "Man exists not on the boundary between God and creation, but on a boundary within creation itself: between the *visibilia et invisibilia*, the conceivable and inconceivable, the humanly attainable and the humanly transcendent." The impact of *The Centaur* suggests that, in effect, Peter Caldwell has submitted himself to the attainable facts of his father's human life. The son may have been in his vocation only a second-rate abstract expressionist painter, but in his avocation he has become a first-rate representational artist, who, in the verbal contours of Greek pastoral elegiac myth, has sketched a beautiful and useful and transcendent truth.

Peter creates a beautiful and transcendent truth, but it is useful because it is also experiential. It is on this point that one must finally take issue with Vargo's fine essay on *The Centaur*. There are several problems one must point out. The first is simply that he stresses too much the form of the novel as rite or ritual. To the extent that it is formalized as a *thing done* the novel may constitute a ritual action, but in that case every work, every poem, becomes a rite since all can be defined as symbolic actions. Consequently, in this case "rite" is clearly less useful a term than "myth," for myth suggests better than rite the verbal, the imaginary, dreamlike quality of the work and its locus in a mind. The critical superiority of myth becomes clear when Vargo states that "The chief function of ritual in this novel . . . is to serve as an action against death." But the novel, instead, is no imagining of an action; it is an imagining of an imagining, an introjection, an emotional assimilation of the fact of death. The novel seems far less a rite than a cry, an utterance, an expression of love, grief, and consolation. A second problem is that even myth proves less useful as a means for understanding the novel when Vargo suggests the order by which meaning is attributed to it. Vargo writes, "By its transformation of a particular situation into a paradigm, myth makes rite dynamic and meaningful. Without it, ritual is an empty shell." The movement of the novel, however, suggests that the basic, meaningful term is neither rite nor myth, but *experience*. Rite cannot give meaning to experience, nor can myth, but experience can infuse and give substance to rite and myth. To make myth primary is to discount the concrete fact of George Caldwell in Peter's experience. For Peter, as, apparently, for Updike, existence precedes essence, the flesh precedes the world, and it is Peter's imagining of his father's life and death that makes possible the sacral universe of which Vargo speaks and through which man can make contact with God. Art is finally the only answer to the eschatological questions Peter raises. Aesthetics becomes the eschatology. It is finally the Art of Peter's expression that transmutes experience and creates—as perhaps by definition, every new work of art must—a new myth for his time.

The Centaur is an elegy, not upon the death of a friend, a leader, or a god, but upon the death, real or imagined, of a man's father. As a lyrical expression of grief and love, this novel comes close to the spirit of a poem like e. e. cummings's "my father moved through dooms of love." Like cummings's poem, Peter's is a celebration of a father's life, an act of atonement for the suffering that the father endures in his life. Cummings's poem says his father has moved through conformity ("sames of am"), selfishness ("haves of give"), indifference ("dooms of feel"), and alienation ("theys of we"); Peter's says his father has moved through "Waste, rot, hollowness, noise, stench, death," "the many visages which this central thing wears." But cummings's poem concludes with the kind of affirmation that seems possible to a man in the face of that furthest thing known as death:

> because my father lived his soul
> love is the whole and more than all

Peter's elegiac expression comes to a similar conclusion, and it comes directly out of his own and his father's experience. Knowing now he is not going to die momentarily from the cancer he had feared, George Caldwell feels at the end "that in giving his life to others he entered a total freedom." As if this revelation also allows him to regain the innocent world of total, resonant metaphor, George is then cast as a mediator, as a meeting place wherein the forces of life can regenerate themselves: "Mt. Ide and Mt. Dikte from opposite blue distances rushed toward him like clapping waves and in the upright of his body Sky and Gaia mated again." In his body, that grotesque medium formed from man and beast, the wasteland he might have bequeathed to his son is revivified. And the beautiful, useful, transcendent truth of Peter's art is revealed: "Only goodness lives. But it does live." The most satisfying of the beauties of this truth, coming as it does from a celebration of a son's love for his father, is the fact that it is the *father's* father, George's father, who evokes it in the first place. The novel suggests not the biblical notion that the *sins* of the fathers are visited upon the sons, but the more benevolent idea that it is the wisdom of the fathers that is passed along. The novel's form thus contradicts George Caldwell's repeated mutterings about his inheritance only of "a Bible and a deskful of debts." It clearly contradicts his feeling that he will pass on to Peter only a message of despair. The elegiac form Peter creates finally expresses more than a son's personal feeling; it expresses a reverence for life and a faith in the continuity of the human spirit. All this is what the novel as lyric elegy can achieve—does indeed fully achieve in *The Centaur.*

JANE BARNES

John Updike: A Literary Spider

In 1979, two collections of John Updike's stories appeared, *Too Far to Go*, published in February by Fawcett, and *Problems*, published by Knopf in October. Rather than review these books by themselves, I want to discuss the stories in the new collections that round out one distinct phase of Updike's involvement with themes of family life. It is a phase which began with the Olinger stories and which follows a single narrator through his adolescence, marriage, and divorce. From story to story, this narrator appears in slightly different guises—his name changes, he lives in different towns or cities. Of course, not all the narrators of all the stories are this narrator; but from the Olinger fictions to the most recent ones, certain traits of character and key repetitions from a particular life story identify several heroes as one man.

To a great extent, the tension in these stories derives from the conflict between the illusions fueling the adult from the past and the demands made on him as a parent and husband in the present. His childhood hopes, desires, dreams are frustrated by family life, and Updike's narrator is constantly turning back—less and less, however, to rediscover his childhood's glory. As he passes through his cycles of hope, discouragement, and liberation, his childhood becomes the text which he earnestly studies for clues to who he is and what he should do and how he got into his situation in the first place. Over the twenty or so years during which Updike has published stories, much of the drama has been generated by the narrator's changing view of his relation to his mother and father, as well as the changing way he regards their marriage. In fact, his first

From *Virginia Quarterly Review* 57, no. 1 (Winter 1981). © 1981 by *Virginia Quarterly Review*.

marriage seems largely undertaken in imitation of his parents'. The narrator's slow coming to terms with his unhappiness in the marriage, his falling in love, and gradual accumulation of the nerve to act (to divorce and remarry)—all these occur because of revisions in his understanding of the past.

II

In the early Olinger stories, during the narrator's boyhood, he is subject to the willful, frustrated, hard-working adults who roam the house like lions pacing the narrow dimensions of their cage. The narrator is a gifted only child who is both admired and excluded by his contemporaries. Within his family, a once prosperous group who've fallen on hard times, his talents give him a special role. His mother's parents and his parents share a large house; suppressed furies make it feel small, and the boy's sensitivities pick up every last feathery vibration of the conflicts binding the adults. From the start, he is also conscious of his mother's urging him to take advantage of his gifts, to fly, to escape the fate she has suffered.

In "Flight," the narrator looks up from the newspaper while he is reading to his grandfather.

> It would dawn on me then that his sins were likely no worse than any father's. But my mother's genius was to give the people closest to her mythic intensity. I was the phoenix. My father and grandmother were legendary invader-saints, she springing out of some narrow vein of Arab blood in the German race and he coming over from the Protestant wastes of New Jersey, both of them serving and enslaving their mates with their prodigious powers of endurance and labor. For my mother felt that she and her father alike had been destroyed by marriage, made captive by people better yet less than they. It was true my father loved Mom Baer, and her death made him seem more of an alien than ever. He, and her ghost, stood to one side, in the shadows but separate from the house's dark core, the inheritance of frustration and folly that had descended from my grandfather to my mother and me, and that I, with a few beats of my grown wings, was destined to reverse and redeem.

It is worth quoting this passage at length because so much that unravels in the later stories is tied here in intricate knots. Updike's narrator returns repeatedly to these key elements: his understanding that his mother and father are unhappily married, that his mother is the larger spirit of his two parents, that his father represents virtue, and that he, the boy, is divided between them. As a boy, while he is still his mother's son, his sense of division is not as intense as it becomes in later years, after the narrator has married and is himself a father.

But during his own boyhood, he tailors himself to her unconscious demands. Several stories contain variations on the boy's sense that his mother is not happy, "that the motion that brought us again and again to the museum was an agitated one, that she was pointing me through these corridors toward a radiant place she had despaired of reaching." Repeatedly, the mother in these stories thirsts for culture for her son. Sometimes this drive is recollected ironically, so that she appears as a kind of no-nonsense improver—a sort of Carrie Nation of the mind; but, more frequently, the mother is the muse of transcendence, a destination which she believes, however vaguely, however wrong-headedly, can be reached through art. For her son, she is the first woman to be associated with art, but afterwards, women and art will represent the mysteries he wants most to understand.

In fact, Updike did grow up to be an artist, and though there is probably an autobiographical connection between the author and his central narrator, the important thing here is to settle what is set forth in the fiction. In terms of the narrator's profession, things are rather shadowy, as if his job were of third or fourth importance in his life. In one story, the narrator has "a job teaching mathematics to ex-debutantes at a genteel college on the Hudson." In another, he is an "assistant professor at a New Hampshire college." In "Wife-Wooing," the narrator's job is a poetic composite of all men's work. "Stone is his province, the winning of coin. The maneuvering of abstractions. Making heartless things run. Oh the inanimate adamant joy of jobs!" Richard Maple, the narrator of the central series of stories about a marriage that fails, commutes to an unnamed occupation. Like all the other narrators, Richard Maple's primary task is not business, but self-awareness. More than that, his first responsibility is to know the *meaning* of life; what he should do, how he should live.

For this man, women are the carriers of the mystery within which meaning may lie. His various, not to say conflicting, desires for them create the moral problem he struggles to solve. Yet when he marries, he marries young (long before he has had any real experience with women), and he chooses someone who is both "better and less" than he. "She was a fine-arts major, and there was a sense in which she contained the museum, had mastered all the priceless and timeless things that would become through her, mine as well. She had first appeared to me as someone guarding the gates." With one difference, the wife's limiting or critical relation to the narrator is almost exactly what he perceived his father's was to his mother. The difference is that his wife's superiority is one of class, as if he'd understood all his mother's urgings as a simple plea to climb the social ladder. Still, the effect of his wife's upper class is like that of his father's virtue, and in one of its manifestations (civic duty), is exactly the same. It is impossible not to feel that the narrator is repeating the pattern of his parents' unhappy marriage. He seems to be taking on his mother's suffering, in part because he identifies with her and does not want some pleasure she will never have herself. He assumes her suffering out of a desire to solve it, so that he might find an answer both of them can use.

However, once the narrator becomes a father his interest in his own father begins to increase, if not actually to shift away from his mother. The boy in the Olinger stories saw his father as a "ditherer." The young father regards the same man as a "potential revelation" and competes with his wife "partly in the vain hope of the glory his father now and then won in the course of his baffled quest." But this rising identification also complicates the narrator's sense of his role in his marriage. The closer he comes to his father—the more, in other words, that he is conscious of his responsibility—the more trapped he feels. As his sense of being forced to match his wife's virtue increases, his sense of diminishment waxes proportionately. He has not solved the suffering in his parents' marriage; he has repeated it.

The level of domestic irritation begins to rise. "He felt caught in an ugly middle position, and though he as well felt his wife's presence in the cage with him, he did not want to speak with her, work with her, touch her, anything." He begins to be unfaithful, though, at first, this does not involve him in any real conflict. Having lapsed into the familiar unhappy pattern of his parents' marriage, he takes the unhappiness in marriage as an eternal truth. There is nothing to do but pursue what little pleasure one can find (this pleasure, however, brings no real joy because nothing ever really changes) and wait for death. Then everything is suddenly, unexpectedly, and completely altered. He falls in love.

Though his ostensible problem is being torn between his wife and his mistress, this division is the twin of loyalties that were originally torn between his mother and father. On the one hand, romantic love satisfies the raised expectations he received from his mother; on the other, his wife and children have the claim of duty, a claim raised in the narrator's estimation by his adult appreciation of his father's strengths. Yet even while love forces the narrator to face his divisions clearly, love also seems to offer a whole new resolution to his conflict. "Seeing her across a room standing swathed in the beauty he had given her, he felt a creator's, a father's pride."

His mistress and the love they share offer him the chance to become the author of his own happiness. Their love is not just a chance to be free, but also to be his own father, his own man. At the same time, the narrator in love identifies himself with "the creator," the artist, and says that "in this museum I was more the guide; it was I who could name the modes and deliver the appreciations . . . I had come to the limit of unsearchability. From this beautiful boundary I could imagine no retreat."

He may not retreat, but for a long time he is unable to move forward. A series of stories reveals the narrator as lacking either the nerve, the passion, or perhaps the cruelty necessary to leave his wife. The love, which at first offered a clear alternative to his unhappiness, begins to subside, some of it actually seems to slosh back into the marriage—as if his emotions were like the water on the floor of a rocking boat. Though he does not act, he does seem changed, lovingly released in a new way. Nonetheless, while his love spreads out to the world in general—to his wife, his mistresses (he seems to start to have many again), his children, his dog—he still has not satisfied his specific yearning. He is much happier, but his life again becomes static. Once more, his conflicts are so well-balanced that he is paralyzed.

During this period, which stretches through several years, his memories of his childhood begin to serve a new purpose. In the Olinger stories, the narrator's childhood seems to be recollected out of a nostalgia for the past, and in the interest of drawing the original battle lines that marked the little boy's character. In the later stories, once the central crisis of the narrator's marriage has occurred, the stories about childhood seem to go in search of some liberating insight. And in "Solitaire," the narrator finds what he is looking for. He has always regarded his parents' marriage as a difficult one, but he had never doubted its solidity. Having seen their perseverance as a support to himself, as a standard to meet and an example to follow, he comes to see how he kept them together, not they him. In "Solitaire," the narrator plays cards and remembers his mother playing the same game years before.

> He knew now that her mind had been burdened in that period. Everything was being weighed in it. He remembered very faintly— for he had tried to erase it immediately—her asking him if he would like to go alone with her far away, and live a new life. *No*, must have been his answer, *Mother don't* . . . And she, too, must have felt a lack of ripeness, for in the end she merely moved them all a little distance, to a farm where he grew up in solitude and which at first opportunity he left, a farm where now his father and mother still performed, with an intimate expertness that almost justified them, the half-comic routines of their incompatibility. In the shrill strength of his childish fear he had forced this on them; he was, in this sense, their creator, their father.

The narrator is forced to recognize how he literally kept his parents married, requiring them to stay together on his account. (The echo of this is heard in

"Avec La Bebe-sitter," after the narrator has fallen in love with another woman; he and his wife agree to stay together "for the children's sake.") But the more important understanding which comes out of this reexamination of the past is that he sees himself as his parents' "creator, their father." The Freudian logic or compulsion, tactful and twice-removed as it is in these stories, collapses as the narrator assumes the imaginative responsibility for his parents. All along, they have been *his* fictions, and insofar as he has imitated or denied them, he has relinquished crucial authority. But that is just the point: in seeing how the knot is of his own intellectual making (and not a hard, universal law), the narrator frees himself from the binding psychoanalytic tie. "Solitaire" ends: "He was a modern man, not superstitious even alone with himself; his life must flow from within. He had made his decision, and sat inert, waiting for grief to be laid upon him."

After this, the narrator slowly pulls away from his marriage, though as he arrives at his decision to divorce, he once more sees less and less difference between his wife and mistress. In "Domestic Life in America," a story from *Problems*, coming home after a visit first to his wife and then to his mistress, the narrator is struck by the time 10:01 (and temperature 10°: things are the same and their sameness is repeated infinitely). Like his women, the hours and minutes are perfect mirror opposites. But the tone of the story is different from the defeated tone of earlier stories when the narrator saw unhappy marriage as the unchangeable human condition. Though the narrator now sees himself as driven back and forth between two sets of equally draining demands, one of the women (his mistress) gives him something he wants. She offers him sexual happiness, and, finally, he has reached a point where he regards himself as free to choose on the basis of his desires, whatever they are.

In the end, the influence his mother has on his life has declined to the extent that the once overpowering, magical fulfillment she urged him toward has become sexual contentment. At various times, Updike has represented sex as glorious or lost or the only alternative to the death of religion. In "Domestic Life in America," sex is a simple human connection which makes him feel more at home on earth. He has come to choose this because he has given up on the morality that belongs to his wife and father. Yet he does not escape judgment. The virtue which he has found so frustrating in his wife, that very quality which made his father both "better and less" than his mother, that same virtue has the last word. His wife and father have been good, but diminishing, reducing life so it will be small enough for virtue to cover neatly its complexity. But what this means is that, by the narrator's own definition, embracing the complexity is both vital and immoral.

In "The Egg Race," another story from *Problems*, the narrator goes back to a high school reunion where a classmate says, "You aren't half the man your father was." The narrator agrees. His father has emerged from the past as the real hero by whose standards Updike's narrator feels he has failed. In "The Egg Race," the narrator speaks of having left his wife for another woman: "He had long contemplated this last, but would never have done it had his father been alive." Though he's made his way out of the charmed circle of the childhood world he shared with his parents, they have clearly left their mark on the shape he finally assumes. The individual he becomes actually unites his parents again, but in a form that declares his separation, his distinctness. He chooses the path his mother wanted for him, the road to a happier life, but by doing so, he leaves her behind. At the same time, he goes against the example set for him by his father (who, after all, stayed with his wife), and so always knows how he is fallen. I recently read in an essay by Freud that a very long labor will cause the imprint of the mother's pelvic bone to be impressed on the baby's skull; I can't think of a better analogy to describe the influence of his parents and their marriage on the final form of the narrator's character.

III

As the narrator comes to view himself as the author of his parents' marriage, so the author of the narrator seems increasingly to write out of a simple, coherent core. Both books of short stories published in 1979, *Too Far to Go* and *Problems*, demonstrate how fully fledged the author's understanding is of his narrator's place in his domestic world. *Too Far to Go* collects all the Maple stories, the first of which was written in 1956. None of them suffers from the stylistic excesses that mark other stories—as if the Maple series were the best stories from any given stage of Updike's developing perception. At each stage, Updike has written many stories about the insight of that stage, but the Maple stories represent his most polished statement. An exception to this is "Domestic Life in America" in which the narrator is named Fraser, though everything else about his life—his divorce, his wife, children, mistress—are straight out of Richard Maple's résumé, including the clarity of the story's style.

Because of the purity and sureness of the writing, the Maple stories are a clear medium for the narrator's moral dilemmas. The medium is rendered clearer still by the fact that the Maples' experience is considered all by itself, in terms of Richard and Joan and their children. The stories about the narrator's most romantic passion are not written through or for Richard Maple; yet it is known throughout the series that he has had love affairs, and he ultimately leaves Joan for another woman. Tonally, the stories are dominated by the itchy, loving irritation of Mr. and Mrs. which can't include the wilder reaches of emotion. That life swells in secret, and I make the assumption that the unhappily married

narrator in the stories about a raging love affair is actually Richard Maple step-
ping outside his marriage. This is an assumption based on the differences and
limitations of tone. The tone of the Maples' domestic affection outlaws lyricism
in a literary as well as an emotional sense. Yet Richard seems to benefit from the
experience of other narrators, which is why I imagine they are all one man.

But there are other links between the Maple series and the wider exploration of all of Updike's stories about marriage, family, and adulterous love. In
Too Far to Go, the central problem between man and wife is sex. He wants it
more than she does (sometimes it seems she doesn't want any). His sexual frustration, in its most profound implications as "unlived life" (Lawrence's phrase),
reminds us of the unhappiness which allied the younger narrator with his mother.
In *Too Far to Go*, Richard Maple's frustrated longing meets Joan Maple's cool
reserve much as in the Olinger stories the mother's restlessness collided with the
father's more temperate nature. Like that father, Joan is both "better and less"
than Richard; his slow advances toward freedom and love identify his journey
with the narrator, who realizes his mother's dream against his father's restrictions.

In the first story in *Too Far to Go*, "Snowing in Greenwich Village," that
dream exists as the young husband's niggling lust for a woman dinner guest.
In "Here Come the Maples," the last story in the collection, the couple gets
divorced. Richard has fought for his desires and won, though it means failing his
father even as he sheds him. Richard says to his eldest son, after he has told the
boy about the separation, "I hate this. *Hate* this. My father would have died
before doing it to me." In the course of the collection, what starts as weakness,
slyly acknowledged, becomes a transforming force. The Maple's disagreement
about sex is, in the end, a debate between the claims of society and the claims of
the self. For a long time, Joan's side—the former—has more power in the
marriage because she has rules to go by and Richard has not.

There are times when this makes her less appealing than her husband. In
Too Far to Go, two stories specifically contrast her virtue with his irresponsibility
—"Giving Blood" and "Marching through Boston." Both are about her insistence on doing something for people they have no real personal connection with
and his sense of being deprived of her most important affections. "Marching
through Boston" is a comic masterpiece about Joan's involvement with the 1960s
Civil Rights Movement. Despite a bad cold, Richard goes with her to a march in
Boston, gets a worse cold, and comes home wildly raving, " 'Ah kin heeah de
singin' an' de banjos an' de cotton balls a burstin' . . . an' mebbe even de what
folks up in de Big House kin shed a homely tear or two. . . .' He was almost
crying; a weird tenderness had crept over him in bed, as if indeed he had given
birth, birth to his voice, a voice crying for attention from the depths of oppres-
sion." His charm carries the day; he wins the story hands down. Joan gets no
points in the reader's heart, despite the fact that she is out saving the world.

In other stories, Richard's attunement to the "life that flows within" makes him quite awful. For one thing, in the earlier stories, he is hopelessly ambivalent. This compares badly with Joan's prim, but unswerving commitment to duty. In "Twin Beds in Rome," Richard's move toward and retreat from divorce are emotionally exhausting to no avail. The lust which troubled him at the start of the marriage has graduated to love, but the fact that he addresses it to his mistress *as well* as his wife seems self-indulgent. Joan's dutifulness is clear, constructive, restful. In "Waiting Up," Richard's dependence on his wife's virtue is actually disgusting. The story describes him waiting for Joan's return from an encounter with Richard's mistress and *her* husband. It's not exactly clear what the encounter was supposed to accomplish, but it was deliberately planned and executed in a thoroughly grown-up way. Possibly its purpose is for Joan to smooth over the social awkwardness of the affair having been discovered. In any case, the meeting doesn't change the situation. At the end, Richard persists in wanting both women, and the fact that he does makes us prefer the claims of society in the form of Joan over the claims of the self in the form of this selfish vascillator.

About halfway through *Too Far to Go*, it has become obvious that both of them have lovers. We have to assume that Joan's adultery is at least partially retaliatory, but regardless of what drives her to it, the fact that they are both having affairs and both know it brings them equally low. At first, in "Your Lover Just Called," there is a little spurt of intimacy and rediscovery which comes with Richard's first realizing that Joan is attractive to other men. This accelerates in "Eros Rampant" when he learns that she has also been involved in complete love affairs. Finally, however, in "Red-Herring Theory," they seem more petty than racy. They bicker about whom the other is really sleeping with. Joan's red-herring theory is that he pretends to be interested in one woman as a way of drawing attention from his real mistress of the moment. Set after a party, the story is as gritty as the overflowing ashtrays the Maples are cleaning up. The reader longs for one of these characters to make some sweeping, noble gesture, to renounce something, anything—even if it's just to give up smoking. In this story, they seem to have been endlessly treading the same dirty water, both of them, getting nowhere, stirring the same pain round and round and round.

Just as we lose patience with their problems, a new spiritual strength appears in their relationship. They pass beyond sexual discontent and competition. In "Sublimating," they actually decide to give sex up between themselves (and thus to stop arguing about it). Other lovers are still in the background, but there is new clarity to Richard and Joan's characters—like windows which have just been washed. This sharpness does not bring them closer together. In fact, in "Nakedness," the last story before the Maples tell their children they are separating, various bodies are stripped, but all that's exposed is Richard and Joan's individual loneliness within the marriage. We don't know about Joan, but Richard's thoughts about his mistress have a loving, solid—one might say husbandly—ring. His encounters with his wife are hollow. He nurses his insults about her in the privacy of his thoughts. " 'My God,' Joan said, 'It's like Masaccio's *Expulsion from the Garden.*' And Richard felt her heart in the fatty casing of her body plump up, pleased with this link, satisfied to have demonstrated once again to herself the relevance of a humanistic education to modern experience." If he once loved her for her erudition, he now no longer does.

"Separating," another excellent story, does not surprise us with its news about the end of the Maple's marriage. It is remarkable as a revelation of Richard's changed character. He has altered slowly through the stories, but here he emerges, speaking with real authority. He has mixed feelings of love and guilt, hope and regret, but he no longer slides back and forth between the two poles of his ambivalence. He has made a decision in favor of the woman he really wants. As cruel irony would have it, his self-assertion robs his wife of the support of everything she's stood for. When he leaves her, Joan's virtue does not keep her warm. In "Divorcing: A Fragment," she has lost her control; she is miserable; she begs him to come back after a year and a half of separation. There is the horrible suggestion that without a self to suppress, duty hasn't got a leg to stand on. It turns out that her virtue was just her form of selfishness, her method of keeping her husband. It was also her way of denying him, as his self-assertion is his way of denying her.

At the end of the collection, their roles are reversed. "Here Come the Maples" is the story of the couple's moment before the judge. Richard's values are triumphant. He knows what he wants and insists that his wife play by his rules. Joan is as fragile and accommodating as her young husband had once been when she was the keeper of the social order. If only because the author takes sides, lavishing his gifts on Richard's subtleties, we do, too. In the course of time, Joan will probably make a comeback as the world's most wonderful person, but at the end of *Too Far to Go*, we feel that Richard's upper hand is more than just a win. It seems like a step in the right direction of freedom, truth, and love.

IV

Updike seems to write the way spiders spin: weaving his webs to catch life as it passes, spinning, spinning as much to survive as to astonish. He is probably the most prolific gifted writer of his generation, though the quality of his outpouring is uneven. The problem of picking and choosing between what is good and what is less good is related, I think, to his subject. As a rule, the stories about the particular narrator I have described seem to be better than Updike's other stories. These others fall into several categories: experimental ("Under the Microscope," "During the Jurassic"), descriptive ("The Indian," "Son"), and — for lack of a better word — journalistic ("When Everyone Was Pregnant," "One of My Generation," "How to Love America"). All of these stories have in common the absence of such literary conventions as character, plot, or dialogue. They seem to serve the purpose of unburdening the author's receptive mind of all the different kinds of information that he breathes in from his environment.

What distinguishes the stories about the narrator is the emotion irradiating the finely spun structures. They are more truly felt than the experimental or journalistic stories which seem too much like demonstrations of the author's facility with language and data. At the same time, the stories about the narrator also vary; between the earliest stories and the most recent ones, while the narrator is struggling to come to terms with sex and love, the style is often puffy, sometimes it seems downright anxious — as though the author were really not sure of the material. In the course of Updike's development, the problem of meaning has been complicated by and interlocked with the problem of handling his talent. At moments, he seems to have been swept away by sheer youthful delight, as though his gift were a marvelous toy; other times, a terrible piety seems to have possessed him, as though he could only live up to his promise by taking his Style seriously. And then his intelligence, along with his remarkable observing powers, presented real problems by crowding his attention with an embarrassment of impressions, details, facts.

These distractions get the upper hand when the author's moral grasp of his material is weakest. In "Packed Dirt, Churchgoing, A Dying Cat, A Traded Car," for instance, the overwriting goes hand in hand with the falsely ancient tone of the young man. He comes home to see his sick father in the hospital, his thoughts coated by a world weariness worthy of a very old person who'd seen nothing but war, torture, and death. In fact, the narrator is a young, suburban husband who's seen nothing but peace and domesticity, whose real problem (as he confesses to a hitchhiker) is that he doesn't see the point of his virtuous life. This is not quite the same thing as confronting the void, though there is a tendency in Updike's stories to inflate American boredom into French existentialist despair. At his worst, there is more sneakiness than evil in Updike, more opportunism than moral questing in his restless, curious narrator.

Then, too, though the narrator is clearly a self-centered person, it is not clear that his suffering is more than the pinch we all feel trying to live decently with others. His suffering sometimes seems like pure whining — his philosophizing nothing more than a complaint that spouses can cramp a person's sexual style. It is generally assumed that Updike's stories about domestic life are autobiographical. This assumption seems to be made out of a worldly wisdom which allows all sophisticated people to connect what is known about the author through articles (*i.e.*, that Updike has been married, divorced, and recently re-married) and what happens in the fictional life of his central hero (who has been married, divorced, and recently remarried). It *is* hard not to wonder if the narrator hasn't benefited from Updike's possible experience. At the start, the narrator is a timid, even a cowardly man. That he slowly, but surely has his way with women probably has less to do with a change in his personal charm and more with the unadmitted fact that the author's fame made him desirable and gave him unexpected opportunities, ones which Updike passed on to his narrator. There are times when the narrator's cheerlessness about his adulteries seems just insupportable, only explicable by something having been left out—such as the fact that this is not the typical experience of a lusty suburban male, but rather the typical experience of a celebrity who suddenly finds himself in sexual demand. The narrator's depression would be more believable if it *were* openly identified as the cynicism a famous author might feel towards a rise in his desirability that had nothing to do with his true human self.

Yet having made these criticisms, I want to disassociate myself from the knowing, worldly assumption that Updike's work must be autobiographical. I want to consider the role of autobiography in these stories, but I want to do it from the inside out. Instead of talking about them as reflections of the author's life, I want to discuss their importance in his development as a writer.

Updike himself makes the connection between the human content and the author's art. He speaks of his hero's sense of being the "creator" of both his parents and his mistress. From the start, we know the narrator regards women and art as equally mysterious, if not equivalents. We know that women have dominated his experience, that they are the media through which he comes to terms with the past, learns to love and begins to act for himself. When the author refers to the narrator's sense of himself as the artist of his private life, the association of women with art naturally teams up with Updike's identification with his hero. We can take this as the primary, the *essential* starting point of any discussion of the role of autobiography.

Having begun, there are several paths open to us, all leading to "Domestic Life in America" as a culmination of the art the author has evolved through his hero's quest. Through time, the resonance in these stories has deepened, the authorial voice has become true, simpler, wiser. As a collection, *Problems* is marked by the author's growth as a writer, but the best stories in the book are best because they are about the subject which is most crucial to Updike. In those, form and feeling are one; the problem raised and the problem solved matter because the human heart is at stake; the drama is literally tied to it like a creature punished in the flames.

The narrator is not that complicated a character, but he seeks complexity out. As he has explored the varieties of erotic experience and conflict, Updike's style has reflected the alteration in values and depths and types of feeling. The best Olinger stories provide us with a model of what Updike's recent stories have returned to. In "Flight," "Pigeon Feathers," "A Sense of Shelter," there is more fancy writing than there is in *Too Far to Go* or *Problems*, but in both groups of stories the writing all serves a purpose. In the long run, the unruly impulses in his style seem to have been brought under control by the same principle that liberates the narrator from the past.

"His life must flow from within." As the narrator clarifies his values, as he becomes his own man, free of his ties to the past, Updike's style becomes simpler again. In "Domestic Life in America," there are few unnecessary words, almost no irrelevant descriptions. There is a very clean-cut relationship between content and art, between the narrator's inner state and the story's language and design. In fact, it is a photograph of the narrator's feelings at this moment in his life, yet the story has more power than this description of stasis might imply. It has the power of Updike's best writing—his quick insight, wit, and catlike tread. I associate this purity of style with another source of power in the story: it reveals a new resolution of conflicts which the narrator has been wrestling with from the start.

"Domestic Life in America" describes Fraser's visit to his estranged wife and two of their children, followed by a trip to his mistress's household. The parts mirror each other like two halves of an inkblot. Though there are different people in each place, they present the same degree of difficulty. Fraser's guilty relationship to his own children is no better than his problematic relationship to his mistress's offspring. The reminders of death he finds at his first wife's do not go away when he goes to his next wife's. At the first, he is involved in the burial and emotion attending the death of their dog, a yellow Labrador. As he arrives at his mistress's house, he sees her pinching mealybugs off her plants and killing them. It is almost a tie between the trade-offs each woman involves. The wife, of course, has claim to his guilt; but in her intelligence, her nonchalance under pressure, her decisiveness, Jean also seems personally more attractive than Fraser's mistress. Gerta is rather vulgar, though humorous, and much more selfish than the woman he has left for her.

The sexual pleasure Fraser finds with his mistress is compared to the pleasure he always got coming home from work and diving into the channel beside his land. "It was as when, tired and dirty from work, Fraser had stripped and given himself to that sustaining element, the water in the center of the channel, which answered every movement of his with a silken resistance and buoyed him above its own black depth." While this comparison shows yet another similarity between the two households, it also contains the essence of their difference. There is pleasure for him in both places; and that pleasure has something to do with the unconscious (underwater) life of the senses. But his first wife contributes to this satisfaction only insofar as she is an aspect of his property. If she were all he had, he would have lost what made him happy as her husband. Though he owns nothing with his mistress, though he is actually a trespasser on her property (the gift of her husband), still Fraser is happy with her.

The equations between one household and the other mount as the story progresses, culminating in Fraser's glimpse of the time and temperature as he returns to Boston: 10:01 and 10°. The perfection of this image sets the drama in final clarity before us, recalling the whole history of the narrator's problem even while it casts this dilemma in a new form. The series of numbers demonstrates the similarity between the narrator's choices, but as the witness he is also another actor—one who can and does tip the balance.

Originally, the narrator was paralyzed because every action involved a life-and-death struggle. He could not move without moving against someone else. For the young narrator, identification with one parent meant attacking the other. For Richard Maple, giving his wife her way meant giving up his own. Finally, however, the narrator is compelled to act because not acting hurts himself. No one else is going to act on his behalf; he has to. But for him to reach this point the problem has had to change. The extreme either/or that characterized the important people in his life has subsided. The narrator slowly but surely has incorporated into himself the parts of his parents which, at first, he served alternately as absolutes. He takes his own shape, and as he does, the opposing principles in the universe around him cease to clash so violently. The sense of futility so often present in the early stories is transformed, not because the problem goes away, but because the narrator has become engaged in it. "Domestic Life in America" is there as proof. The narrator is alive and well by virtue of his willingness to pursue what he wants. He has accepted the fact that this will hurt others, and does what he can to take responsibility for his part in the dog-eat-dog reality. He cannot change his feelings, but he does not hide or suppress them. While he also fulfills his obligations at the level of finances and work, the most important form his responsibility takes is acting on what he perceives to be "the real relation between things."

This last is from Marx, who also said that people would only know what these real relations were once they had rid themselves of their illusion. Through time, the narrator's illusions have worn away, allowing the difficult, tiring, moving human truth to emerge. The relationships which have had various kinds of power over the narrator turn out to be commanding for the simplest reason. These people, after all, are not the symbols he once envisioned. They are just the people he happened to know in life. He probably would have known them anyway, even if they had not fit into his sense of how the world was divided.

Division has haunted the narrator and informed the writer's art. It grew out of the boy's understanding of the differences between his parents and grew into his conflict between marriage and wife, on the one hand, and love and mistress, on the other. For some time, the division between parents and women was also between duty and self, morality and pleasure. In "Domestic Life in America," the element of compulsion, of one thing versus another, has fallen away. There is still strife and conflict, but it is between characters who are both good and bad, who are as mixed as the blessings they enjoy and the penalties they pay. The arguments which the narrator worked out through them were always only partially true about the human beings. And the real debate was always one the narrator was having with them about his own nature.

CYNTHIA OZICK

Bech, Passing

I love John Updike (*agape*, not *eros*). When some time ago in *Commentary* Alfred Chester (my old classmate, who vanished into Algiers and then died in Jerusalem) flicked Updike off as a magician of surfaces, I wrote in my head the imaginary counter-review: Updike as Late Church Father. For years I sniffed after an opportunity to think in print about the sacral Updike, and now that the chance is palpably here, it turns out to be not *Pigeon Feathers*, or *Rabbit, Run*, or *The Centaur*, or *Of the Farm*, not even *Couples*: those fictions of salvationism and eucharistic radiance. Instead, *oif tsulokhes* (the phrase of regret Bech's Williamsburg uncles would use and toward which Bech is amnesiac), here is Henry Bech, Jew, rising, like Shylock and Bloom, out of a Christian brain.

Updike, whose small-town stories in particular have suggested him as our most "American" writer, is considerably less American, it seems to me, than, say, George P. Elliott or R. V. Cassill, secularists in a post-Christian neuterland. It is not especially American to be possessed by theology, and Updike is above all the Origen of the novel. The epigraph for *The Poorhouse Fair* is from Luke, *Couples* is emblazoned with Tillich, *Rabbit, Run* quotes Pascal concerning "the motions of Grace." In *Couples*, as in Saint Theresa, love's arrows and Christ's thorns fuse: "He thinks we've made a church of each other," someone says of one of the couples at the start, and in the last chapter fellatio becomes the Sacrament of the Eucharist: "when the mouth condescends, mind and body marry. To eat another is sacred." Further rich proofs and allusions will contribute nothing: it is already well-known that John Updike is a crypto-Christian, a reverse Marrano celebrating the Body of Jesus while hidden inside a bathing suit. (Vide "Lifeguard,"

From *Art and Ardor*. © 1983 by Cynthia Ozick. Knopf, 1983.

Pigeon Feathers.) Even Bech, a character, as they say, "pre-processed"—even Bech, who doesn't know much, knows *that*. In a letter that constitutes the foreword to *Bech: A Book* (this letter, by the way, wants me to call it "sly," but I am too sly for that), Bech tells Updike: "Withal, something Waspish, theological, scared, and insulatingly ironical . . . derives, my wild surmise is, from you." The original Marranos, in Spain, were probably the first group in history to attempt large-scale passing. As everyone knows (except possibly Bech), they ended at the stake. So much for Jews posing. What, then, of Christian posing as Jew? What would he have to take on, much less shuck off?

In the case of Updike's habitation of Bech, nothing. Bech-as-Jew has no existence, is not *there*, because he has not been imagined. Bech-as-Jew is a switch on a library computer. What passes for Bech-as-Jew is an Appropriate Reference Machine, cranked on whenever Updike reminds himself that he is obligated to produce a sociological symptom: *crank, gnash*, and out flies an inverted sentence. Not from Bech's impeccably acculturated lips, of course, but out of the vulgar mouth ("Mother, don't be vulgar," Bech says in boyhood) of a tough Jewish mother lifted, still in her original wrap, straight out of *A Mother's Kisses*. The foreword—which, like all forewords, is afterthought and alibi—tries to account for this failure of invention by a theory of the Comic: it is, you see, all a parody: ironically humorous novelist Bech addresses ironically humorous novelist Updike and coolly kids him about putting Bech together out of Mailer, Bellow, Singer, Malamud, Fuchs, Salinger, the two Roths. The Appropriate Reference Machine is thereby acknowledged as the very center of the joke; the laugh is at the expense of the citation. In search of a Jewish sociology, Updike has very properly gone to the, as Bech would say, soi-distant Jewish novel. And found:

Category: *Vocabulary*
  1. Adjective: *zoftig*
  2. Nouns
     a. *shikse*
     b. *putz*
  3. Ejaculation: *ai*

Category: *Family*
  1. Beloved uncles in Williamsburg
     a. back rooms
     b. potatoes boiling, "swaddled body heat"
  2. Father (mentioned twice in passing)
     a. uxorious, a laugher
     b. no occupation given

3. Mother
   a. buys Bech English children's books at Fifth Avenue Scribner's
   b. takes young Bech to awards meeting of facsimile of Academy of Arts and Letters

Category: *Historical References*
1. "the peasant Jews of stagnant Slavic Europe"
2. Russian "quality of life" "reminiscent of his neglected Jewish past"
3. "Hanukkah"

Category: *Nose*
Bech's: Jewish big
(Forgive this. An in-joke. Updike's, *goyish* big, earns him the right.)

Category: *Hair*
Bech's: Jewish dark curly

Category: *Sex*
1. Sleeps willingly with Gentile women; like Mailer (though a bachelor) tries out whole spectrum of possible *shikse* types
2. But invited to sleep with *zoftig* Ruth Eisenbraun, is less willing; unclear if he does or doesn't

All right. No quarrel with most of these attributes. If the only Yiddish Bech knows is *shikse, putz,* and *zoftig,* he is about even with most indifferent disaffected de-Judaized Jewish novelists of his generation. And I suppose there are Jewish novelists who, despite the variety in the gene pool, have *both* big noses *and* kinky hair: one (affectionate) stereotype doesn't make an anti-Dreyfusard. And if, on a State Department-sponsored visit, Bech associates the more comfortable tones of Russia—"impoverished yet ceremonial, shabby yet ornate, sentimental, embattled, and avuncular"—with his "neglected Jewish past," his is, like that of other indifferent disaffected de-Judaized Jewish novelists, a case not so much of neglect as of autolobotomy. Emancipated Jewish writers like Bech (I know one myself) *have* gone through Russia without once suspecting the landscape of old pogroms, without once smoking out another Jew. But because Bech has no Jewish memory, he emerges with less than a fourth-grade grasp of where he is. His phrase "peasant Jews" among the Slavs is an imbecilic contradiction— peasants work the land, Jews were kept from working it; but again Bech, a man who is witty in French, who in youth gave himself over to Eliot, Valéry, Joyce, who has invented a comic theory of the intelligence of groups, who thinks of himself as an Aristotelian rather than a Platonist — this same Bech is a historical cretin. If there had been "peasant Jews" there might have been no Zionism, no State of Israel, no worrisome Russians in the Middle East . . . ah Bech! In your uncles' back rooms in Williamsburg you learned zero: despite your Jewish nose and hair, you are — as Jew — an imbecile to the core. Pardon: I see, thanks to the power of Yuletide, you've heard of Hanukkah.

So much for the American Jewish novelist as sociological source. As a subject for social parody, it is fairly on a par with a comic novel about how slavery cretinized the black man. All those illiterate darkies! Bech as cretin is even funnier: they didn't bring him in chains, he did it to himself under the illusion of getting civilized.

Nevertheless a few strokes seem not to be derivative and may be Updike's alone: one, the whimsical notion that a woman who speaks sentences like "Mister Touch-Me-Not, so ashamed of his mother he wants all his blue-eyed *shikses* to think he came out from under a rock" would venture past Gimbels to any Fifth Avenue store, much less to Scribner's for English (*English!*) children's books. Having adequately researched P.S. 87, Updike might have inquired at the neighborhood branch library for Bech's sweaty-fingered, much-stamped ancient card ("Do Not Turn Down the Leaves"). Updike's second wholly original misapprehension is a descent into inane imagination. Comedy springs from the ludicrous; but the ludicrous is stuck in the muck of reality, resolutely hostile to what is impossible. That this same woman would by some means, some "pull," gain entry to a ceremony in a hall of WASP Depression *Hochkultur* is less mad than the supposition that she would ever have gotten wind of such doings. What rotogravure section carried them? Bech's mother's culture drive stops at the public-library door; Bech goes in without her, and if he ends up reading Hawthorne in Bulgaria, the credit belongs to P.S. 87. Bech's grandfather's mind came equally unfurnished: what produces a Bech is a grandfather just like him, with no conscious freight of history, no scholarliness, and the sort of ignorant piety of rote that just sustains against poverty. Remove the poverty, slip in P.S. 87, and you have Bech.

What Updike leaves out (and what Roth puts in) is the contempt of the new Bech for the old Bechs: the contempt of just appreciation. Updike writes, "all the furniture they had brought with them from Europe, the footstools and phylacteries, the copies of Tolstoy and Heine, the ambitiousness and defensiveness and love, belonged to this stuffy back room." (For love's duration in close family quarters, see Roth, supra.) Footstools in steerage? From out of the cemeteries on Staten Island, ten thousand guffaws fly up. The beds left in Minsk still harbored the next wave to come. The phylacteries they threw away at the first sight of a paycheck for pants-pressing. And those who read Tolstoy or Heine alighted not in New York but in Berlin. Or stayed behind to make the Revolution. A Jew who came to New York with some Gemara in his brain was absolved from spawning Bech. Bech is a stupid Jewish intellectual. I know him well.

I am not asking Updike to be critical of Bech—it is not his responsibility: it is mine and Bech's. Besides, Updike loves Bech too much, especially where (and this is the greater part of the book) he is thoroughly de-Beched. Updike can be as funny as Dickens and as celestial as bits of *Anna Karenina*, and in *Bech: A Book* he is, now and then, in glimpses, both. This happens when he is forgetting to remember about Bech-as-Jew; luckily, the crunch of the Appropriate Reference Machine is sometimes silenced. Updike loves Bech best when Bech is most openly, most shrewdly, most strategically, most lyrically Updike. Bech's failure— he is a celebrated writer suffering from Block—is rumor and theory, but the exact flavor of Bech's success is the stuff of Updike's virtu. Who else but Updike could take fame so for granted as to endow it with exhaustion? The exhaustion is examined with Updike's accustomed theological finesse: Bech's Block is to be taken somewhat like the modern definition of the Christian hell—no fire and brimstone in a fixed nether location; instead a sense of irreparable loss, a feeling of eternal separation from God, a stony absence of Grace. In the presence of his Block, Bech becomes christologized. In the wilderness of his London hotel lobby he is even subjected to satanic wiles: the devil is a young journalist named Tuttle into whose notebook Bech spills his spiritual seed:

> Bech talked of fiction as an equivalent of reality, and described how the point of it, the justification, seemed to lie in those moments when a set of successive images locked and then one more image arrived and, as it were, superlocked, creating a tightness perhaps equivalent to the terribly tight knit of reality, e.g., the lightning ladder of chemical changes in the body cell that translates fear into action or, say, the implosion of mathematics consuming the heart of a star.

Imagine the Body of Christ describing its transubstantiation from bread. What could the devil do but flee that holiness? But then, coming ever closer, there approaches the ghostly clank of the A. R. Machine, and the eucharistic Bech folds flat and begins to flap like the leaf of an ethnic survey-analysis study:

> He said, then, that he was sustained, insofar as he was sustained, by the memory of laughter, the specifically Jewish, embattled, religious, sufficiently desperate, not quite belly laughter of his father and his

father's brothers, his beloved Brooklyn uncles; that the American Jews had kept the secret of this laughter a generation longer than the Gentiles, hence their present domination of the literary world; that unless the Negroes learned to write there was nowhere else it could come from; and that in the world today only the Russians still had it, the Peruvians possibly, and Mao Tse-tung but not any of the rest of the Chinese. In his, Bech's, considered judgment.

Here Updike, annoyed at the Machine's perpetual intrusions, allows it to grind itself into giggling berserkdom. The Machine is amusing itself; it is providing its own ethnic jokes. (The inopportune demands of Bech's Jewishness on his author should serve as sufficient warning to other novelists begging to be absorbed uninterruptedly by epiphanies: beware of any character requiring more sociology than imagination.) Bech, confronted at last by the journalist's printed report of their encounter, guesses the devil's spiritual triumph over matter: "He [Bech] had become a character by Henry Bech." Which is to say, a folk character out of Jewish vaudeville, not quite Groucho Marx, not yet Gimpel the Fool. Nevertheless unsaved. But while none of Updike's people has ever attained salvation, salvation is the grail they moon over. Bech's grail is cut in half, like his name, which is half a kiddush cup: *becher*. Over the broken brim the Jew in Bech spills out: Updike, an uncircumcised Bashevis Singer (as Mark Twain was the Gentile Sholem Aleichem), is heard in the wings, laughing imp-laughter.

The center of *Bech: A Book* is a sustained sniff of this Christian hell: it is so to speak an inverted epiphany, a negative ecstasy. Bech lectures at a southern girls' college and experiences a Panic: "He felt dizzy, stunned. The essence of matter, he saw, is dread. Death hung behind everything." He sees "the shifting sands of absurdity, nullity, death. His death gnawed inside him like a foul parasite." "All things have the same existence, share the same atoms, reshuffled: grass into manure, flesh into worms." "The grandeur of the theatre in which Nature stages its imbecile cycle struck him afresh and enlarged the sore accretion of fear he carried inside him as unlodgeably as an elastic young wife carries within her womb her first fruit." The abyss swells and contracts, until finally it shrinks from Immense Void to empty *becher* and again becomes recognizable merely as Bech's Block: "He tried to analyze himself. He reasoned that since the id cannot entertain the concept of death, which by being not-being is nothing to be afraid of, his fear must be of something narrower, more pointed and printed. He was afraid that his critics were right. That his works were indeed flimsy, unfelt, flashy, and centrifugal. That the proper penance for his artistic sins was silence and reduction." It is typical of Updike that he even theologizes writing problems, though here he parodies his standard eschatology with an overlay of Freudian theodicy. The fact is Updike theologizes everything (in *Rabbit, Run* he theologized an ex-high-school basketball player); this is his saving power, this is precisely what saves him from being flashy and centrifugal. The stunning choice Updike has made—to be not simply an American but a Christian writer—distinguishes him: in this he is like a Jew (though not like Bech): America as neuter is not enough.

But he does not theologize the Jew in Bech. In seven chapters (really separate stories) he takes the mostly de-Beched Bech everywhere: from Russia to Rumania and Bulgaria, through scenes sweated with wistful wit and ironic love; from a worshipful pot-smoking ex-student through a shift of mistresses; from Virginia to stinging London to a sophomoric "Heaven" where the "Medal for Modern Fiction was being awarded to Kingsgrant Forbes" while the "sardonic hubbub waxed louder." (This last section, by the way, need not be compared for satiric force with Jonathan Swift: I suspect because both the Jewish Appropriate Reference Machine *and* the Literary Politics A. R. Machine, in tandem, were working away like *Mad*.) Wherever Updike is at home in his own mind, the book runs true, with lyric ease: the jokes work, small calculations pay off, anticlimaxes are shot through with a kind of brainy radiance. Without Bech, *Bech* might have been small but sharp, a picaresque travel-diary wryly inventing its own compunctions. But wherever the Jew obtrudes, there is clatter, clutter, a silliness sans comedy. Bech makes empty data. It is not that Updike has fallen into any large-scale gaucherie or perilous failures-of-tone. It is not that Updike's American Jew is false. It is that he is not false enough.

By which I mean made up, imagined, mythically brought up into truthfulness.

In the case of Bech—and *only* in the case of Bech—Updike does not find it worthwhile to be theological. In no other novel does he resist the itch of theology; everywhere he invests ordinary Gentile characters with mythic Christian or proto-Christian roles, adding to local American anthropology a kind of sacral sense. And when the sacral is missing, sulphur drifts up from the Void. Updike is our chief Dante: America is his heaven and hell. He has no such sense of Bech. It is as if he cannot *imagine* what a sacral Jew might be. You might want to say he is not altogether to blame, after all: what would any accurate sociological eye see on the American landscape but Bech? Nevertheless Bech is deviation, perhaps transient deviation, from the historical Jew. Being historical cretin, Bech does not know this about himself: unable to inherit his past, he has no future to confer. He is very plausibly without progeny: though his writing Block is an Updikean Christian salvational crisis, his Jewish Block consists in being no longer able to make history. As Jew he is all sociology, which is to say all manners (acquired exilic manners); as Jew he is pathetically truncated, like his

name. So Updike finds Bech and so he leaves him. Updike comes and goes as
anthropologist, transmuting nothing.

It is very queer—it is something to wonder at—that Updike, who is always
so inquisitive about how divinity works through Gentiles, has no curiosity at all
about how it might express itself, whether vestigially or even by its absence or
even through its negation, in a Jew. Being a Jew (like being a Christian) is
something more than *what is*. Being a Jew is something more than being an
alienated marginal sensibility with kinky hair. Simply: to be a Jew is to be
covenanted; or, if not committed so far, to be at least aware of the possibility of
becoming covenanted; or, at the very minimum, to be aware of the Covenant
itself. It is no trick, it is nothing at all, to do a genial novel about an uncove-
nanted barely nostalgic secular/neuter Bech: Bech himself, in all his multiple
avatars (shall I give you their names? no), writes novels about Bech every day. It
is beside the point for Updike and Bech together to proclaim Bech's sociological
there-ness. Of course Bech is, in that sense, there. But what is there is nothing. In
a work of imagination Bech-as-he-is is critically unjustifiable. It is not Bech-as-
he-is that interests us (if you want only that, look around you), but Bech-as-he-
might-become. If to be a Jew is to become covenanted, then to write of Jews
without taking this into account is to miss the deepest point of all. Obviously
this is not Updike's flaw exclusively; it is, essentially, the flaw of the Jewish
writers he is sporting with. It is no use objecting that Updike and others do not
aim for the deepest point: concerning Jews, the deepest point is always most
implicated when it is most omitted.

Descending, for the sake of the Jew alone, from the level of theological
mythmaking to the level of social data, is Updike patronizing his Jew? One
thinks, by contrast, of a Jew writing about a Gentile: I mean *Henderson the
Rain King*. Meditating on the quintessential *goy*, Bellow makes up a holy culture
to demonstrate him. The demonstration is not through *what is*, but through
opposites: the *goy* is most revealed as not-Jew. It seems to me that a Christian
writing of a Jew would profit from a similar route in showing the quintessential
Jew as not-Gentile. Whereas Bech has no inner nature of his own, and only
passes. Or I think of a short story, not altogether seamless but divinely driven,
by George P. Elliott, in his collection *An Hour of Last Things*: a Jewish woman
fevered by the beauty of a cathedral is made to waver between revulsion for
Christian history and the lustful leap into the idolatry of Art. Here a secularized
post-Christian WASP writer explores the most awesome, most dangerous, most
metaphorical depths of Commandment.

Two questions, then, remain to puzzle. Why, for Bech, does Updike with-
hold his imagination from the creation of Bech *as Jew*? And second: what motive,
what need, what organic novelistic gains, emerge from the turn to Bech? As some

say Mailer taunted Updike into the sexual adventurism of *Couples*, so now, it is declared, a similar competitiveness with Jewish "domination of the literary world" (Bech's self-sneering Gaullist phrase) compels him to a Jewish character. I reject the competitive motive: it seems plain that Updike experiments for himself, not for other writers, and pits himself against values, not persons. But while *Couples* turned out to be a Christian novel, *Bech* is a neuter. It may be that Updike's experiment this time lies precisely in this: to attempt a novel about no-values, about a neuter man. To find the archetypical neuter man, man separated from culture, Updike as theologian reverts to Origen and Ambrose, to centuries of Christian doctrine, and in such ancient terms defines his Jew. If the only kind of Jew Updike can *see*, among all these cities and hearts, is Bech, that is not solely because Bech is in the majority, or most typical; it is because for him Bech—the Jew as neuter man; the Jew as theological negative and historical cipher—is most real.

But seen from the perspective of the Jewish vision, or call it Jewish immanence (and what other perspective shall we apply to a Jew?), the Jewish Bech has no reality at all, especially not to himself: he is a false Jew, a poured-out *becher*, one who has departed from Jewish presence. For Updike to falsify the false—i.e., to lend the Jew in America the Grace of his imagination—would have been to get beyond data to something like historical presence, and a living Bech. But that, I suppose, would have required him to do what Vatican II fought against doing: forgive the Jew for having been real to himself all those centuries, and even now. And for that he would have had to renounce the darker part of the Christian imagination and confound his own theology.

POSTSCRIPT

Bech: A Book is followed, a dozen years later, by *Bech Is Back*. The tone of the sequel is greatly refined; for one thing, Updike has junked the Appropriate Reference Machine. Bech, left to himself, ethnic banners banned, sociology damned, vestigial Yiddish reduced to two unspoken grunts (alas, they are the words for "whore" and "unclean"), elegantly comic mind almost everywhere beautifully conflated with Updike's own—Bech lives. In *Bech Is Back*, Bech is, by and large, no more a Jewish character than I am a WASP. This satisfies him; if his newest success—a bestseller called *Thinking Big*—allows him the time, I hope he will write Updike a thank-you letter, especially since, as it turns out, there is only one bad patch for the ethnic Bech to get through: a visit to what the chapter-title, in wall-map Sunday-school language, terms "The Holy Land." This pilgrimage is undertaken in the company of Bea, Bech's Episcopalian wife, all pure responsive essence, whose name (even if accidentally) is metaphysically interesting in context. In Israel, only Bea can rapturously, serenely, supremely, Be; Bech cannot. He moves in this consecrated landscape as a skeptic and an antago- nist; and here, to be sure, Updike has precisely nailed the post-Enlightenment intellectual Jewish scoffer epitomized by surly Bech—for whom, after the Nazi depredations, after the Arab wars, "events in Palestine had passed as one more mop-up scuffle, though involving a team with whom he identified as effortlessly as with the Yankees." Only the last part of this judgment rings false; Bech is non-, perhaps anti-, Zionist, and always was.

The "Holy Land" section opens in Jerusalem not, as one would expect, with a trip to the lost Temple's Western Wall, sighed after for two thousand years of teary Exile, but with a walk, led by a Jesuit guide, along the Via Dolorosa. Still, Bech must not be credited with making a beeline for the very spot that stands, in every Passion Play, and annually at Eastertide, for the historic revilement of "perfidious" Jews; it is Updike's walking tour he is taking, not his own. The controversial lands west of the Jordan River are designated, tenden- tiously, as "occupied territory" (whether in Bech's or Updike's head, or both, it is difficult to tell), a characterization by no means linguistically immaculate or politically neutral. (Perhaps Bech, when he gets back home, will write an attack on the Begin government's settlement policy for *The New York Times Magazine*.) The Western Wall itself appears as the Wailing Wall, an antiquated christological insult. Bech and Bea are put up at a lavish government guest house for distin- guished visitors, "echoing," thinks Bech, "like the plaster-board corridors of a Cecil B. DeMille temple," where he is tempted to cavort like Bojangles on the wide stairs. The "tragic, eroded hills of Jerusalem" just beyond those corridors, and the brilliant Valley of Gehenna a breath's space below, do not draw Bech's eyes or his hardened heart. The holiness of the Holy Land leaves Bech cold; only his Gentile wife catches its heat. In deference to Bea's touching ardor—the ardor both of the romantic tourist and of the industrious Christian pilgrim—Bech visits the City of David dig, the two shining mosques atop the Temple Mount, and, among squabbling sectarians, the arena of Bea's generous surrender to spirit, the Church of the Holy Sepulcher. Bech's raised anti-Israel consciousness is not disappointed at a dinner with Israeli writers "in a restaurant staffed by Arabs. Arabs, Bech perceived, are the blacks of Israel." Finally, when Bea, honoring Bech's Jewishness, proposes moving to Israel to live, Bech retorts: "Jesus, no. It's depressing. To me, it's just a ghetto with farms. I *know* these people. I've spent my whole life trying to get away from them, trying to think bigger." Later he will visit the land of Bea's forebears, and find "happiness in Scotland." He will defend the Highlanders against their historic oppressors. He will be amazed and amused, edified and electrified, in Ghana, Korea, Venezuela, Kenya, Canada, Australia. Only in Israel is he depressed.

Thus, slippery, satirized, satirical Bech. Does Updike mean Bech to mean what Bech says? Does Bech say what Updike means? In his second coming, returned briefly to Jewish scenes, Bech is, as Jew, not really Redux. As Jew he merely momentarily recurs, as reduced—as reductive—as before. Nothing can transform him; he will not be elevated, even by the holy heights of Jerusalem. His secular skepticism will not be contradicted by any whiff of the transcendental; he is the only major character in Updike's fiction wholly untouched by the transcendental. He remains man sans spirit, no different from that medieval Jew whom Christendom deemed hollow, unable to be hallowed: theological negative in Jerusalem, historic cipher in Zion, carper in the precincts of Ariel. As scoffer and Jewish neuter, Bech is, yes, "real," "actual," "lifelike," abundantly "there." Updike's curled irony has not ironed him out; I recognize him. "I *know* these people," as Bech would say. As a symptom of a segment of Jewish reality, Bech is well and truly made.

Charles Dickens sold his house—it was called Tavistock House, and you will see how I am not changing the subject—to a certain Mr. J. P. Davis, a Jew. According to Edgar Johnson, Dickens's biographer, Davis's wife Eliza

> wrote Dickens a letter telling him that Jews regarded his portrayal of Fagin in *Oliver Twist* as "a great wrong" to their people. If Jews thought him unjust to them, he replied, they were "a far less sensible, a far less just, and a far less good-tempered people than I have always thought them to be." Fagin, he pointed out, was the only Jew in the story (he had forgotten the insignificant figure of Barney) and "all the rest of the wicked *dramatis personae* are Christians." Fagin had been described as a Jew, he explained, "because it unfortunately was true of the time to which that story refers, that that class of criminal almost invariably was a Jew. . . . I have no feeling towards the Jews but a friendly one," Dickens concluded his letter.

I believe Dickens; he is the best and most honorable of geniuses. I certainly believe that he believes he is telling the truth. There *is* a curious point, though, in the choice of Fagin's name. When the boy Dickens lay, so to speak, in the miserable pit of his childhood, crushed and seemingly snuffed forever by his forced employment in a warehouse, beaten up by the other boys for his "airs"—the early signs, no doubt, of the miracle he became—only one fellow-worker took pity on him, cared for him, and was consistently and deliberately tender to him. That boy's name was Bob Fagin. We know with what unkind immortality the warehouse of Dickens's unconscious repaid that first Fagin.

A quarter of a century after the completion of *Oliver Twist*, Dickens obliged Eliza Davis with an act of literary compensation: he invented Mr. Riah of *Our Mutual Friend*. Mrs. Davis wrote to thank him. Some time afterward she presented him with a Hebrew Bible. Dickens again commented, "I would not

wilfully have given an offence or done an injustice for any worldly consideration."
He had already let Riah speak for him: "Men say, 'This is a bad Greek, but
there are good Greeks. This is a bad Turk, but there are good Turks.' Not so
with the Jews. Men find the bad among us easily enough—among what peoples
are the bad not easily found?—but they take the worst of us as samples of the
best; they take the lowest of us as presentations of the highest; and they say 'All
Jews are alike.' "

Bech, it seems to me, is, as Jew, not the best or the highest. Since he is
caricature, it will not do to have him best or highest: comedy is ill-served by
loftiness. Nor is Bech, funny and fond and woeful and brave, a literary (prepos-
terous thought) Fagin. Still, what if Updike followed Dickens in turning his Jew
upside down—or, rather, in allowing him to rise? As Fagin is extravagantly
lurid, so is Riah extravagantly gentle. There is a comedy in that, though unwit-
ting: the innocent purposefulness of undoing one caricature in order to make
another. Compensation snickers; restitution is risible.

It is ten years from now. The third book in the delightful series (and for the
occasion the binding is not "perfect" but sewn) is called *Bech, Bound* (in Hebrew: *Bech, Baal-T'shuvah* [Tel Aviv: Sifriat Hapoalim, 1992]). Whither is
Bech bound? What is his destination? And what, above all, is binding Bech? The
memory of Moriah, Isaac's binding. The thongs of the phylacteries. The yoke of
the Torah. The rapture of Return. The dictionary meaning of "ethnic." (In
Bech's beat-up old *American College Dictionary*, from college, this surprise:
"pertaining to nations not Jewish or Christian; heathen or pagan; as, *ancient
ethnic revels*.") By now Bech has read his Bible. He has been taking Hebrew
lessons; he is learning Rashi, the eleventh-century commentator whose pellucid
explications even little children can understand. Bech, as Jew, is like a little child,
though pushing sixty. Akiva too began to study late. Starting with the six-
volume Graetz, bound in Jewish Publication Society (Philadelphia) crimson,
Bech has mooned his way in and out of a dozen histories. He is working now on
the prayer book, the essays of Achad Ha-Am, and the simpler verses of Bialik.
He seeks out the Chancellor of the Seminary for long talks. He is reading Ger-
shom Scholem.

Bech stands on a street in Jerusalem. The holy hills encircle him—they
are lush with light, they seize his irradiated gaze. He is, for the first time,
Thinking Big.

What will Updike, honorable and resplendent mind, do with such a big
Bech?

DONALD J. GREINER

The Coup

All the languages they used, therefore, felt to them as clumsy masks their thoughts must put on.

—The Coup

Nearly everyone agrees that *The Poorhouse Fair* is an unusual first novel. How, admiring readers asked in 1959, can an author so young write about people so old? With the dash and assurance of an experienced novelist, Updike reversed the normal procedure of first purging himself with a story of youth and initiation and offered instead a tale of age and belief. *The Poorhouse Fair* is an extraordinary debut.

Just as unexpected as the subject matter was Updike's decision to set his first novel in the near future. Many beginning authors write to find out where they are, but Updike took a guess at where we will be. His guess was uncannily accurate. From the safety of hindsight, it is easy to lament the degeneration of handcraft to plastic, belief to busyness; for shoddiness was not so pervasive in the late 1950s when he wrote the novel. Even more difficult than the forecasting was the necessity of visualizing a world for the people at the poorhouse fair. Representing a landscape is more conservative than creating one because the author may rely on the touchstone of familiarity to keep his readers aware of the setting. *The Poorhouse Fair* is not a conservative novel, just as Updike is not always a traditional novelist. Yet to manipulate the conventions of conservative storytelling is not to insist on the excesses of experimental technique. A writer does not have to resort to pyrotechnical displays of narrative energy to illustrate his delight in innovation. One of the triumphs of *The Poorhouse Fair* is that

From *John Updike's Novels.* © 1984 by Donald J. Greiner. Ohio University Press, 1984.

Updike sets his tale in the strange future and yet keeps his readers in touch with the familiar present. The created landscape seems oddly representational. Such is also the case with *The Coup* (1978), his most surprising novel to date.

The mythical future of the poorhouse gives way to the manufactured country of Kush, but in both cases Updike has gone beyond looking around him to imagining the idiosyncrasies of his created worlds. The result in *The Coup* is a sophisticated comedy of language and disguise. Ask the literate reader to define the normal concerns of Updike's novels, and he is likely to suggest suburbia, adultery, and the crises of middle age. He will be correct. Rabbit Angstrom may not be welcome at the cocktail parties in Tarbox, but he can sympathize with the long-legged wives and the intrigues there. Conversely, Colonel Ellelloû suffers enough grief from his wives and mistresses to understand the pathos and absurdities of both Rabbit and Tarbox, but his tale is not one of suburbia. Middle-class comfort and available lovers may be at the periphery of his problems, but the mystical integrity of Kush occupies the center. The point is that *The Coup* is a change of pace in the Updike canon.

Most commentators recognized the shift in locale and emphasis, and Joyce Carol Oates noticed it better than anyone else. In an essay that praises the novel while indicating its intricacies, she calls *The Coup* "a lengthy monologue that really *is* a coup of sorts, constituting Updike's most experimental novel to date." Oates understands that *The Coup* is as different as *The Poorhouse Fair*, and she correctly insists that while Updike pays homage to Vladimir Nabokov with a virtuoso command of style and voice, he does so without Nabokov's "self-referential props": "the prose Updike has fashioned for [Ellelloû] is even more difficult and resembles nothing so much as an arabesque superimposed upon another arabesque. Motifs, phrases, 'imagery,' coarsely comic details from the 'external world,' Ellelloû's various and conflicting pasts, are rigorously interwoven into complex designs."

As might be expected, not everyone agrees, especially *Commentary*. It makes no difference whether Updike publishes in the late 1950s or the late 1970s; *Commentary* is ready for the attack. Such foolish consistency loses its sting as the attacks drag on with the years, but followers of Updike's career usually check out the *Commentary* review to see what new bases for disparagement the editors have found this time. Pearl K. Bell's essay-review avoids the personal harangue and hysterical tone of past analyses of Updike in *Commentary*, but, of course, her evaluation is finally negative. She admits that the novel is "audacious" and that Ellelloû is a "great achievement," but she mistakenly assumes that Updike tries to write in "blackface" and thus fails to "close the gaps between his alien sensibility and the obdurate reality of Africa." Such a comment ignores Ellelloû's education in America. A graduate of McCarthy College in Franchise, Wisconsin, he is not likely to write with the metaphors and rhythms of a Kush tribesman. Even more questionable, Bell realizes that the reader should not make the common error of identifying an author's "moral attitude" with that of his characters, but she then turns around and accuses Updike of a "hackneyed caricature" of America even though the comic diatribe comes from Ellelloû: "In its scornful parody of American culture, *The Coup* is clearly a descendant, a particularly simplistic descendant, of that recurrent illusion of paradise."

Harold Hayes, Maureen Howard, Deborah McGill, and Dean Flower also worry about voice. Although most commentators praise the astonishing twists and turns of Ellelloû's sardonic memoirs and bewildered meditations on "the idea of Kush," Hayes argues that the Colonel's language "too blissfully transcends the reality of character." In a word, Hayes wants realism, the kind that will teach him something about African dictators, and thus he is unhappy with Updike's imagined locale. Similarly, Howard wants Updike to write like Nabokov or Conrad, and she decides that the voice of the novel is "all Updike." Deborah McGill hears not Updike in Ellelloû's rhythmical confessions but, incredibly, Jerry Conant, the hero of *Marry Me* (1976). While many readers laud Updike's discovery of Kush, McGill finds that he never leaves suburbia where absolution is unearned, guilt rarely assigned. Finally, in an extremely negative commentary, Dean Flower attacks *The Coup* for lacking conscience, indulging its style, and preaching from the point of view of a narrator who sounds like "every other Updike anti-hero."

One can only grant these readers their say and then reply that Ellelloû does not sound like Updike or his other characters. Surely Rabbit Angstrom cannot speak with the Colonel's rhythm or imagination; he is too busy trying not to grow old in his middle twenties. The same goes for Joey Robinson (*Of the Farm*, 1965), who may be more speculative than Rabbit but who does not come within an unabridged dictionary of Ellelloû's command of language. *The Coup* was greeted with many more cries of praise than howls of derision, as suggested by Peter Collier in, of all places, the *Book-of-the-Month Club News*: "It's not so much 'style' that distinguishes this writer as it is a whole way of seeing. He has the quality which T. S. Eliot found in the works of Andrew Marvell: 'a tough reasonableness beneath a slight lyric grace.'"

To blend lyricism with the remoteness of Kush is in itself a kind of coup. As Updike says, "I've always been attracted to hidden corners." Africa was "the emptiest part of the world I could think of." What is so much fun about *The Coup* is that he fills that emptiness with language. To insist on a correlation between Kush and Chad, or to demand that Updike use his African novel to teach us about African dictators, or to require representational language when the whole point of the novel is that language creates its own realities is to miss a delightful, surprisingly funny reading experience, what Robert Towers calls a "comedy of absurd cultural juxtaposition." In Kush the Third World is in collision as much with itself as with the superpowers, and its leader has only oratory in reserve. While the United States sends in McDonald's and miniskirts, and the Soviets send in missiles, Ellelloû sends out metaphors with such a worried face that the reader ends up laughing. The irony is that the Colonel's concern is legitimate, for he confronts a dilemma of either pure Kush and starving Kushites or debased Kush and swinging Kushites. Another irony is that the people of Kush care nothing for purity. The "idea of Kush" has melted with the vapor and the heat, spinning away with the nomads who cross Ellelloû's path, and it may be that, however unfortunate, the people glimpse the future better than the leader. Paul Theroux has a point: "I did not attempt to give a sense of place to my fiction until I wrote about Africa; it helped me see straight. . . . Updike has done a more difficult thing. His Kush is both real and imagined. . . . More important than the Americans who will read this book are the Africans who will at least understand what it is that they have been trying to say."

Unlike Theroux, I am not concerned that *The Coup* will help Africans understand themselves, but I am bothered by Americans who dismiss the novel as an inaccurate representation of the African sensibility. Such charges not only reveal the reader's avoidance of the excitement of imagination for the safety of verisimilitude but also recall the irrelevant outcry against William Styron's *The Confessions of Nat Turner* because Styron had dared to imagine a black leader's mind and to express it in the first person. The task of the novelist is to create a landscape that is true to the needs of his fiction. In this sense Kush is as much an imagined domain as it is a point of departure for Updike's satiric potshots at what John Hook in *The Poorhouse Fair* calls goodness without belief — "busyness." Kush is so destitute, so dispirited, so dry that it is more a state of mind than a nation, but Updike's imagination convinces us of its geography. Who can resist a country that contains ancient caves decorated with a combination of primitive rock-paintings and American graffiti, especially "Happy Loves Candy," the nicknames of Ellelloû and his wife?

The juxtaposition of art and graffiti is one way that cultures collide. War is not an issue in Kush. Yet everywhere Ellelloû turns, he sees both bubble gum and the Koran, hears rock music and the rites of prayer. When he confesses poetically to his wife Candy that he is about to "walk the edge of my fate, and may fall off," she responds as if from another planet: "Don't give me any of this Kismet crap. . . . I knew you when you couldn't tell the Koran from the Sears Roebuck catalogue." Ellelloû is powerless before such bluntness. How can he call on the cadences of language when he knows that his listeners care nothing for words?

As Alastair Reid observes, American colloquialism becomes the "language of the infidel." Updike's insight into global politics suggests that not armaments but words are the keys to invasion. Reid's praise of *The Coup* captures its many facets: "Call *The Coup* a caper, an indulgence, a tract, a chronicle, a fable — and it is all these things at different times — the fact is that Updike's sentences can be read with the pleasure that poetry can, and the fingers are more than enough to count the novelists of whom such a thing can be said."

His sentences come from many sources. Although Updike traveled in Africa as a Fulbright lecturer in 1973, he reveals in a page of acknowledgments that he also journeyed there with the aid of books. Along with a series of scholarly studies consulted for the occasion, he lists *National Geographic*, "children's books, *Beau Geste*, and travellers' accounts." Eclectic reading shapes the background of *The Coup*. Accounts of the 1968–74 drought merge with thrilling tales of the Foreign Legion, and the result is a sardonic commentary on global confusion.

But Updike also used books to travel to Africa before he thought of *The Coup*. As a regular reviewer for the *New Yorker*, he has written essays about such African authors as Yambo Ouologuem, Kofi Awoonor, and Ezekiel Mphahlele. Readers who do not want to track down the separate issues of the *New Yorker* where these and other pertinent essays were published may find them collected under the catch-all title "Africa" in Updike's miscellany *Picked-Up Pieces* (1975). In the essay "Shades of Black," he muses generally on the dilemma that faces Ellelloû in *The Coup*: How does a modern African handle language? Ellelloû is not sure, and while he would not deign to express himself in the pages of the *New Yorker*, he might agree with Updike's understanding of the problem:

> The black African moved to literary expression confronts choices a Westerner need not make. First, he must choose his language — the European language, with its alien tradition and colonial associations, or the tribal language, with its oral tradition and minuscule reading audience. Unless his mother and father came from different tribes and used a European tongue as the lingua franca of the home, his heart first learned to listen in the tribal language, which will forever then be more pungent and nuancé; but English and French command the far broader audience, across Africa and throughout the world. So he must choose his audience: foreigners and the minority of his countrymen educated in white ways, or the majority of his fellow-tribesmen, who can be addressed chiefly through recited poetry and theatrical performance. . . . The African writer must consciously choose not only his language, audience, and tone but his reality.

Language, tone, and reality—these are the stumbling blocks for the Colonel. Audience is not an issue because he writes chiefly for himself, but complexities of tone and language have always affected his wanderings through reality as he tries to juggle Islamic mysticism and Western training. A son of the tribe and a soldier for France, Ellellou is also a student in America and the leader of Kush. No wonder his scheming assistant Ezana describes him as ruling "by mystical dissociation of sensibility." Leaving the practical concerns of running the country to the treaties and plots of those who care, Ellellou quests into the mysterious wastes of Kush in search of a mystical cause of the drought. What he finds is a parody of himself in the guise of a city crammed with the junk he has labored to keep beyond the borders. The city's name? Ellellou.

Thus *The Coup* is more than a comic-strip tale of emerging Africa; it is an imaginative commentary on the ridiculousness of power politics, the idiocies of nationalism, and the infinite recesses of language. The difference between Updike and Ellellou is that the former knows that language is political as well as creative, whereas the latter hopes to separate the two. The Colonel wastes his poetry on glamorous declamations that say, in effect, that America stinks or Russia smells. We know that we have picked up a comic fable about political realities when on the first page we read Ellellou's outrageous rhetoric about the prostitution of Kushite peanut oil to make American soap: "then the barrelled oil is caravanned by camelback and treacherous truck to Dakar, where it is shipped to Marseilles to become the basis of heavily perfumed and erotically contoured soaps designed not for my naturally fragrant and affectionate countrymen but for the antiseptic lavatories of America—America, that fountainhead of obscenity and glut." Or, when the Volvos of "Swedish playboys" "forfeit their seven coats of paint to the rasp of sand and the roar of their engines to the omnivorous howl of the harmattan," Ellellou cries righteously, "Would that Allah had so disposed of all infidel intruders!" But fountainheads of glut and infidel invaders cannot be kept out by rhetoric. Unfortunately for the Colonel, poetic flourishes are all he has. He apparently misses the irony that he spouts the rhetoric of revolution while prowling around Kush in a German Mercedes and worrying about his marriage to an American blond.

Ellellou's joyous command of language is further undercut by our suspicion early in the novel that he is no longer the leader of Kush. Describing the form of government in his country as "a constitutional monarchy with the constitution suspended and the monarch deposed," he must now face the galling truth that he has also been removed. The first clue that a coup has replaced him is the word *here* in the following sentence: "(I am copying these facts from an old *Statesman's Year-Book*, freely, here where I sit in sight of the sea, so some of them may be obsolete)." He does not tell us where "here" is, but he does imply that he is now distanced from the time of his tale.

Narrative distance is a source of irony and laughter in *The Coup*. Writing about a land where even memory "thins," Ellelloû tells his story not to defend his policies but to discover them: "In a sense the land itself is forgetful, an evaporating pan out of which all things human rise into blue invisibility." The people of Kush may think that the Colonel has evaporated, but he still longs to anchor his life. What happened, he wonders. All he has left are language and the past. *The Coup*, the novel itself, will not reinstate his presidency but it will guarantee his memory. So he tells his tale to explain as much to himself as to the reader why he is a victim of a quiet revolution, and he knows that narrative distance is one way to investigate the self: "There comes a time in a man's life . . . when he thinks of himself in the third person."

Although placed late in the novel, this comment is the key to Updike's narrative technique. A student of the Koran, Ellelloû understands sura 76, which Updike uses as an epigraph: "Does there not pass over man a space of time when his life is a blank?" To write his memoirs is to fill the blank, so the Colonel switches, occasionally even in mid-sentence, from third person to first person as a way of indicating both narrative distance and the dual perspective he has of his political career. Needless to say, that career baffles him: "There are two selves: the one who acts, and the 'I' who experiences. This latter is passive even in a whirlwind of the former's making, passive and guiltless and astonished. The historical performer bearing the name of Ellelloû was no less mysterious to me than to the American press. . . . Ellelloû's body and career carried me here, there, and I never knew why, but submitted." The "I" may be passive before the whirlwind of the "he," but the "I" controls the tale of the "he" who acted. All the "I" wants to do now is find out why.

The point is that Ellelloû is a narrator watching his own presence in the story he is narrating. Once, for example, he interrupts the tale to explain that his manuscript is blurred in places by a wet ring from a glass of Fanta. Since he is now drinking such impurities, one wonders about his outburst against American obscenity and glut. The public mask is clearly not the private man when the "I" suffers the effects of the "he's" actions but drinks junk that the "he" would dash to the ground. Ellelloû, of course, claims that not he but Kush acts whenever he declares an outrage or defines a role, but the "I" is not so sure now. After all, Ellelloû has revolutionized a country in which there is nothing to revolutionize. With twenty-two miles of railroad, one hundred seven of paved highway, and two Boeing 727s in Air Kush, this drought-stricken land has little use at the moment for the complexities of ideology and identity. The irony is that Ellelloû prefers the emptiness. While his assistant Ezana negotiates for oil rights and capital, the Colonel fights for mysticism and purity. Money brings meddlers, and meddlers bring modernity, the very things, Ellelloû argues, the country does not need if it is to retain its sense of being Kush. Thus it is revealing when he rants against the American students of the 1960s who only played at revolution, for he knows now that he has also failed to touch the pulse of his people.

Longing to identify with Kush, to see himself as the personification of his country, he plays a series of roles with the various masks he adopts—beggar, singer, laborer—in order to travel the land anonymously: "His domicilic policy is apparently to be in no one place at any specific time." But his determination to know his people by adopting their roles eventually confuses his identity and blinds him to his true relationship with his nation. He can be a tribesman or an Islamic Marxist, but he cannot be both despite his efforts to support tribal purity with revolutionary rhetoric. The closest he comes to knowing who he is occurs when he pays a poignant visit to the Salu tribe and his first wife: "For there lay no doubt, in the faces of these his relatives, that through all the disguises a shifting world forced on him he remained one of them, that nothing the world could offer Ellelloû to drink, no nectar nor elixir, would compare with the love he had siphoned from their pool of common blood." What a comedown from that pool of common blood to a glass of Fanta. He can drop his masks with the Salus, who call him Bini, but while he longs for their serenity, he also dreams of a Marxist paradise in an Islamic nation. The two desires paralyze him. Listening to his wife Kadongolimi point out his flaws, he has no answer to her charge that he has forsaken the gods of their fathers for revolutionary zeal: "Have you forgotten so soon? The gods gave life to every shadow, every leaf. Everywhere we looked, there was spirit. At every turn of our lives, spirit greeted us. We knew how to dance, awake or asleep. No misery could touch the music in us."

Ellelloû begs to believe, but he finds himself pulled between those like Kadongolimi who trust the old gods of nature and those like Ezana who worship the new gods of consumerism. Unfortunately for the Colonel, most of his people agree with Ezana. Disguised as he travels through Kush, Ellelloû watches as rock and roll displaces prayer. The result, he realizes, is not religion in any form—the gods of nature or the gods of the Koran—but entropy:

> in the attenuation, desiccation, and death of religions the world over, a new religion is being formed in the indistinct hearts of men, a religion without a God, without prohibitions and compensatory assurances, a religion whose antipodes are motion and stasis, whose one rite is the exercise of energy, and in which exhausted forms like the quest, the vow, the expiation, and the attainment through suffering of wisdom are, emptied of content, put in the service of a pervasive expenditure whose ultimate purpose is entropy, whose immediate reward is fatigue, a blameless confusion, and sleep.

Ellelloû has certainly not abandoned religious belief to the reward of fatigue, but at the end of the novel he approaches a kind of entropy: His ceaseless quests have left him motionless.

The Colonel's religious fervor is part of his faith in the "idea of Kush." It makes no difference to him that the country was once called Noire, or that it is mired in poverty, or that a plentiful horde of diseases is listed among its natural resources. What matters is his devotion to the spirit of his stumbling nation. He does not want his people to starve, but neither does he want the tentacles of American and Soviet aid to squeeze the land. Given the dilemma, he militantly chooses the former and sets out on his quest to discover a religious source of the drought. Purge the dragon and the land will thrive. But there is no dragon, just as Ellelloû is no St. George. All he can do is publicly execute old King Edumu who reminds the assembled witnesses of the contrast between the abundance during his reign and the disaster during Ellelloû's: "If their rule is just, why has the sky-god withheld rain these five years? . . . I say Kush is a fiction, an evil dream the white man had, and that those who profess to govern her are twisted and bent double. They are in truth white men, though their faces wear black masks." Edumu has a point, for he uncannily sees that Ellelloû models a repertoire of masks. Yet the old king is fighting for his life while the Colonel is struggling for his country. There is little doubt that Ellelloû loves Kush more than Edumu, but the king is cunning enough to throw in the word "fiction" as he denounces his murderer. For Ellelloû's Kush *is* a fiction; no one else has his faith in the mystical power of this wretched land. The final irony is that, for all his devotion, the drought lifts only when he is deposed in a bloodless coup.

All Ellelloû can do is apply to his memoirs the audacious rhetoric that he spouts to his countrymen. Updike, of course, is aware that the rhetorical flourishes in *The Coup* are even more elaborate than those in his earlier novels, and he seems to take a special delight in disturbing the sensibilities of readers who do not share his pleasure in the inventiveness of language. Many of the figurative touches are comic as well as lovely, as when the Colonel describes the king's nose as sitting in "the center of his face like a single tart fruit being served on an outworn platter." In other cases, however, Updike offers self-parody as a way of indicating that the language as well as the landscape of *The Coup* is not rendered but created, made up, a fiction. When Ezana escapes, for example, Ellelloû writes that his assistant makes a series of "knotting, and measuring actions that like certain of these sentences were maddeningly distended by seemingly imperative refinements and elaborations in the middle." Updike jokes of his conscious use of style just as he makes Ellelloû conscious of his intricate twists of narration.

For not Ellelloû but language is the hero of *The Coup*, a source of laughter

as well as a means of defining the masks that condition one's perception of the
world. Recall Updike's analysis of the dilemma facing African authors as they
try to select language, tone, and reality, and then note Ellelloû's description of
his conversation with Edumu:

> They spoke in Arabic, until a more urgent tempo drove them to
> French. All their languages were second languages, since Wanj for
> the one and Salu for the other were tongues of the hut and the village
> council, taught by mothers and lost as the world expanded. All the
> languages they used, therefore, felt to them as clumsy masks their
> thoughts must put on.

Without Wanj and Salu, Kush itself is a fiction; its author is Ellelloû.

The Colonel manipulates language the way he plays with masks, and the
results are unavoidable: His constant donning and discarding of masks and
rhetorical stances confuse his sense of self. He must write *The Coup* to define
not only who he once was but who he now is. The pathos is that he may never
know. Is he the President, the Colonel, Ellelloû, Bini, or Happy? Each name is a
word, and each word is a mask, and the "I" is not sure what to make of them.
When he tries and fails to communicate the reality of the suffering in Kush and
the "cosmic refusal" to prevent it, he is terrified at being stranded without the
protection of a role: "Held mute in a moment without a pose, a mask, Ellelloû
felt the terror of responsibility and looked about him for someone with whom to
share it." But there is no one to share it because no one shares his understanding
of Kush. Even the people do not know who he is.

One of Updike's ironies is that Ellelloû's command of language does
nothing to change his status as little more than a myth in his own country. Some
Kushites have never heard of him, some believe he is a slogan, and some hate him
for being a freed slave, but no one looks to him to end the drought or lift the
famine. Updike's comic touch shapes the narrator's response to his quandary:
"Only I expected this of Colonel Ellelloû." But the passive "I" is only the re-
corder of the active "he's" wanderings. The narrative distance between them is as
unbridgeable as the gap between Ellelloû and the people he does not know.

The highpoint of Updike's suggestion that not arms but language is the
weapon of power politics occurs when Ellelloû confronts Gibbs, the American
do-gooder, before an audience of hungry Kushites. The scene is a set piece of
exaggeration, an inspired blowup of two little men sparring with words in front
of a mountain of American junk food. Battle lines are drawn, stances assumed,
and a war of colloquialisms begins. Gibbs's hip jargon seems insulting before
Ellelloû's rhythmical cadences: "Who're you trying to kid? . . . These cats are
starving. The whole world knows it, you can see 'em starve on the six o'clock

news every night. The American people want to help." Offering tons of dry cereal and powdered milk, the very foods Kush does not need since it has no water, Gibbs personifies America's mindless need to be loved. When Ellelloû points out that America's program of cattle vaccination increased herds that in turn exhausted Kush's limited forage, all Gibbs can reply is that he has read about it in a report: "O.K., O.K.—better late than never. We're here now, and what's the hang-up?"

But while Ellelloû's outrage is justified and his anger at American meddling confirmed, he also resorts to catch-phrases and clichés: "The people of Kush reject capitalist intervention in all its guises. . . . Offer your own blacks freedom before you pile boxes of carcinogenic trash on the holy soil of Kush!" We laugh at his rhetoric even as we understand his fury. Here are two men from different countries who realize that the people of Kush are starving, but while they speak the same language, neither can cross the frontier of words to pose an acceptable solution. Updike then adds another twist to this comic scene when he shows Ellelloû slipping into a different mask that undercuts his sincerity. When Gibbs tells Ellelloû that he once read some of the Colonel's essays in a "Poli Sci course" at Yale, Ellelloû thinks: "So he knew of my exile. My privacy was invaded. Confusion was upon me. I took off my sunglasses. The brightness of the lights shed by the torches was surprising. Should I be getting royalties?" Instead of the righteous defender of his nation, he is now a television star worried about re-runs. He cannot control his masks. With his audience expecting action, he torches both the do-gooder and the junk and inadvertently opens the way for American advisors who will travel to Kush to investigate Gibbs's death.

No wonder a Russian advisor is called Sirin, the penname of another master artificer, Vladimir Nabokov. Ellelloû's ornate use of words is one way that Updike smiles at himself in *The Coup*. Like the Colonel, he dances among flourishes and roles, delightfully playing with variations of prose rhythms and figurative language. But, unlike the Colonel, he is aware of the laughter. Ellelloû takes every conversation seriously, so that while Updike and the reader laugh when Candy calls her husband "the most narcissistic, chauvinistic, megalomaniacal, catatonic schizoid creep this creepy continent ever conjured up," Ellelloû muses on how Americans indulge in "the endless self-help and self-exploration of a performance-oriented race that has never settled within itself the fundamental question of what a man *is*." Satirizing Americanese, the Colonel fails to hear the silly pomposity of his own rhetoric, which hampers his search for an answer to a similar, fundamental question: who is he? The act of writing *The Coup* may tell him.

But it will not tell him what is happening in Kush so long as he avoids reality for mysticism. During his first important journey to the mysterious north, he glimpses two sights that should not be there, a solitary flatbed truck carrying crushed automobiles and odd golden arches that turn out to be a McDonald's hamburger joint. Ellelloû has no idea why they are there, and he would not know how to confront such infidel intrusions even if he could define them. They do not fit with his idea of Kush. Sadly, his people prefer Big Macs and mini-skirts to his notion of purity.

Ezana agrees with them. Identified by his language, as are most of the characters in *The Coup*, he speaks with what Ellelloû calls "the rhetoric of Poli Sci." He is the perfect bureaucrat, a man who sees no need to trek the far wastes of northern Kush in search of mystical explanations for the country's disasters when the lure of American aid is just around the next friendship treaty. For all of Updike's laughter, he recognizes the disintegration of tribal customs and tradi-tional lives if modern men like Ezana assume control. Ezana wants to urbanize the nomads and negate their way of life, arguing that a nation cannot "withdraw into sainthood," but Ellelloû sees only blasphemy in such plans. He realizes that Ezana can produce facts and figures for any situation because the assistant lacks "that inward dimension, of ethical, numinous brooding, whereby a leader bulges outward from the uncertainties of his own ego and impresses a people."

But how does one impress a people if their stomachs are empty and their wells dry? Ellelloû looks for a Marxist explanation for Sittina's hairstyle, while Ezana shifts statistics in hopes of enlisting American money to build offices for Kush's bureaucracy and to translate the Koran into Braille. He will destroy their roots, but he will give them burgers and french fries. Foreseeing not entropy but peace, he argues with Ellelloû that life must be lived in the present:

> The fading of an afterlife—for it has faded, my friend Ellelloû, how-ever you churn your heart—has made this life more to be cherished. When all is said and done about the persisting violence on our planet . . . the fact remains that the violence, relatively, is small, and de-liberately kept small by the powers that could make it big. War has been reduced to the status of criminal activity. . . . This is a great thing, this loss of respectability. . . . Hatred on the national scale has become insincere. . . . The units of race and tribe, sect and nation, by which men identified themselves and organized their youth into armies no longer attract blind loyalty.

What can a linguistic artificer do against such pragmatism? Ellelloû's response that the units of sect and tribe were mankind's "building blocks" and that Ezana's explanation predicts not peace but entropy cannot stop the invasion of flatbed trucks and jukeboxes. Denying religion, war, and nationalism, three un-certainties that Ellelloû believes in, Ezana does not worry about a worldwide drift toward sameness that will eradicate the idiosyncrasies of languages, cultures, and countries. Religious meditation gives way to an "alien rhythm" complete with words "repeated in the tireless ecstasy of religious chant": "*Chuff, chuff, / do it to me, baby.*" The Top Forty has crossed the borders of Kush.

So Ellelloû travels once again to the north, this time to confront the mysterious talking head of the executed king. The journey is his version of the quest, his plunge into the heart of Kush where he hopes to locate the curse and exorcise it. To his surprise but not to ours, since we know that he is writing from the perspective of narrative distance, he finds that *he* is the curse on Kush and that he has already been exorcised. Oil has been discovered in the Ippi Rift, and American plenty in the forms of drilling rights, free beer, and apricot halter tops has ended the drought, restored the land, and indirectly deposed the Colonel. In the wasteland of northern Kush, nearly dying of thirst and heat, he stumbles to a cave that houses not the grail but graffiti. The nuances of language, his primary reserve, cannot sink much lower.

Ellelloû's spiritual self is clearly not pleased when Sirin's Russians rescue his physical body and escort him to the land of the talking head and McDonald's. Feeling a "guilty sensation of something undone, of something disastrous due," he sees the unexpected sight of a "newly built funicular railway" that he does not know is there. His disaster has a quiet irony about it that points back to his eradication of the American Donald Gibbs, for just as the ridiculous Gibbs has been turned into a martyr and will have a library named after him in Kush, so the elegant Ellelloû has been deposed and will have a plastic city named after him—also in Kush. The toppling of the bungling "he" is all too obvious to the observing "I."

The contrast between the Colonel's idealism and Ezana's facts is located once again in language. While Ezana hopes to develop a "plausible pragmatism," Ellelloû travels "westward to the Ippi Rift; but as this new leaf of adventure unfolded before him he felt only an exhaustion, the weariness of the destined, who must run a long track to arrive at what should have been theirs from the start: an identity, a fate." Despite his rhetoric, he finds only a parody of identity: Ellelloû the man comes face to face with Ellelloû the city. The nuts and bolts of Ezana's materialism are everywhere, for when Gibbs dies, a victim of the Colonel's righteousness, all Ezana does is welcome another "Gibbs" with the name of Klipspringer.

Stunned by the go-go city named after him, Ellelloû casts about for a Marxist explanation for what he calls the "blue-collar stink" brought by money. None is forthcoming. Deprived of his identity as president and Colonel, he survives, as always, by dipping into his repertoire of masks: a parking attendant and a short-order cook named Flapjack. The America of his student days has transported itself to Kush, and Ellelloû is back in the confusion of the all-American drugstore with its maze of sunglasses and notions, magazines and cards. All he discovers in his search for identity is that he ceases to exist: "I, submerged in posthumous glory, immersed in the future I had pitted all my will against, relaxed at last."

Just as significant as the expulsion of Ellelloû is the erasure of language. For all along, language has identified both the Colonel and his fears that the modernization of Kush will eradicate the distinctive rhetoric of this unusual land. His fears are justified: "A loss of tension, of handsome savagery, was declared also in their accents, which had yielded the glottal explosiveness of their aboriginal tongues to a gliding language of genial implication and sly nonchalance." Glottal explosiveness and handsome savagery give way to the jukebox of "Cry Me a River" and "A Whole Lotta Shakin' Goin' On," and America wins the war of words without firing a shot. Ezana feels at home with "The Naughty Lady of Shady Lane" and the Donald X. Gibbs Center for Trans-Visual Koranic Studies, but Ellelloû is baffled. Kutunda, his mistress, tells him what we already know: "You have run out of masks."

Exiled to France with a pension, a wife, and his children, he masks himself with NoIR sunglasses and sits by the avenue writing *The Coup*. At the end of the novel, Updike reemphasizes the narrative distance between the teller as he tells the tale and the actor who has acted it: "He does not appear to be the father of the variegated children who march at their sides. . . . It gladdens the writer's heart, to contemplate the future of his girls." Thus Ellelloû observes Ellelloû writing the story; the "I" watches the "he." Holding down a sheet of paper, remembering behind his sunglasses the details of the coup, he retains his audacious rhetorical flourishes and pens "long tendrils like the tendrilous chains of contingency that have delivered us, each, to where we sit now on the skin of the world." Language remains his primary companion, his constant joy. The final sentences call attention not to story but to technique: "The man is happy, hidden. The sea breeze blows, the waiters ignore him. He is writing his memoirs. No, I should put it more precisely: Colonel Ellelloû is rumored to be working on his memoirs." Updike's final comic touch is that Ellelloû is the main character in a novel in which he plays the role of an author writing a memoir in which he is the main character. Such doubletalk is Updike's little joke on his own highly conscious, highly rhetorical art.

The Poorhouse Fair and *The Coup* remain Updike's most unexpected novels. It is not that they are militantly experimental as are John Hawkes's *The Cannibal* or Thomas Pynchon's *Gravity's Rainbow*, or that they transport the reader to such unfamiliar locales as Kurt Vonnegut's Tralfamadore or Robert Coover's Universal Baseball Association. Strangeness is generally not an issue in

Updike's fiction. But for these two novels, this most polished author, long admired for his lyrical discourses on the unhappy bedrooms and rapidly aging lives of suburban Americans, turns from the subject matter that his audience expects and creates landscapes that have little to do with the serious domestic crises of the middle class. The problems of belief in a secular age that rankle the spirits of John Hook and Felix Ellelloû have thematic importance in other Updike fictions, but their significance in *The Poorhouse Fair* and *The Coup* is that they support a perspective on where we are going more than on where we are. Imagining locales that permit him to stand outside, as it were, his familiar fictional territory, Updike invents two settings and the languages that humanize them in order to visualize the drift of the world.

Chronology

1964–65   Updike participates in the USSR-US Cultural Exchange Program and travels to Russia, Bulgaria, and Czechoslovakia.

1965   *Of the Farm* and *Assorted Prose.*

1966   Updike receives O. Henry Prize for "The Bulgarian Poetess." *The Music School* published.

1968   *Couples.*

1969   *Midpoint and Other Poems.*

1970   Updike writes *Bech: A Book.*

1971   *Rabbit Redux.*

1972   *Museums and Women and Other Stories.*

1973   Updike receives Fulbright grant and lectures in Ghana, Nigeria, Tanzania, Kenya, and Ethiopia for three weeks.

1974   Updike publishes a play, *Buchanan Dying.* He separates from his wife and moves to Boston; later they divorce.

1975   *A Month of Sundays* and *Picked-Up Pieces* published.

1976   Updike moves to Georgetown, Massachusetts, and publishes *Marry Me.*

1977   A new edition of *The Poorhouse Fair* published. Updike marries Martha Bernhard.

1978   Updike writes *The Coup.*

1979   *Problems and Other Short Stories* published; *Too Far to Go* published and produced for television.

1981   Updike receives Pulitzer Prize and American Book Award for *Rabbit Is Rich.* Also receives the Edward MacDowell Medal for literature.

1982   *Bech Is Back.*

1983   Updike publishes volume of criticism *Hugging the Shore.*

1984   *The Witches of Eastwick.*

1986   *Roger's Version.*

Contributors

HAROLD BLOOM, Sterling Professor of the Humanities at Yale University, is the author of *The Anxiety of Influence, Poetry and Repression*, and many other volumes of literary criticism. A MacArthur Prize Fellow, he is general editor of five series of literary criticism published by Chelsea House.

JOHN W. ALDRIDGE is Professor of English at the University of Michigan. He is the author of many volumes of criticism including *The Devil in the Fire: Retrospective Essays on American Literature and Culture, 1951–1971, In Search of Heresy: American Literature in the Age of Conformity, Time to Murder and Create: The Contemporary Novel in Crisis*, and the novel *The Party at Cranton*.

RICHARD H. RUPP is Professor of English at Appalachian State University in North Carolina. He is author of *Celebration in Postwar Fiction* and *Getting through College*. He has also written on Hawthorne and Whitman.

DAVID LODGE is Professor of Modern English Literature at the University of Birmingham. His most recent novels include *Changing Places, The British Museum Is Falling Down*, and *Small World: An Academic Romance*. He is also author of several works of criticism including *The Language of Fiction: Essays in Criticism and Verbal Analysis of the English Novel* and *Metaphor, Metonymy, and the Typology of Modern Literature*.

TONY TANNER is a Fellow of King's College, Cambridge. His books include *The Reign of Wonder: Naivety and Reality in American Literature, City of Words: American Fiction 1950–1970*, and *Adultery in the Novel: Contrast and Transgression*. He has also written on Charlotte Brontë, Jane Austen, Henry James, Joseph Conrad, Saul Bellow, and Thomas Pynchon.

JOYCE CAROL OATES teaches in the Department of Creative Writing at Princeton University. A prolific writer and critic, her most recent works include *Expensive People, Invisible Woman, Luxury of Sin, Mysteries of Winterthurn, Marya: A Life*, and the critical anthology *The Profane Art: Essays and Reviews*.

MARY ALLEN is Lecturer in English at George Mason University in Fairfax, Virginia. Her books include *The Necessary Blankness: Women in Major American Fiction of the Sixties*, a work on portrait photography, and a study of animals in American literature.

JAMES M. MELLARD teaches English at Northern Illinois University. He is author of *Quaternion: Stories, Poems, Plays, Essays* and *The Exploded Form: The Modernist Novel in America*.

JANE BARNES is a novelist and critic. She is author of *I, Krupskaya* and *Double Lives*.

CYNTHIA OZICK was a 1982 Guggenheim Fellow and a recipient of the Mildred and Harry Strauss Living Award from the American Academy of Arts and Letters. She is author of *Trust, The Pagan Rabbi and Other Stories, Levitation: Five Fictions, The Cannibal Galaxy, Bloodshed and Three Novellas*, and *Art and Ardour: Essays*.

DONALD J. GREINER is Professor of English at the University of South Carolina. He is author of *The Other John Updike: Poems, Short Stories, Prose, Play* and *John Updike's Novels*, and editor of *American Poets since World War II*.

Bibliography

Backsheider, Paula, and Nick Backsheider. "Updike's *Couples*: Squeak in the Night." *Modern Fiction Studies* 20 (1974): 45–52.

Berryman, Charles. "The Education of Harry Angstrom: Rabbit and the Moon." *The Literary Review* 27 (1983): 117–26.

Brenner, Gerry. "*Rabbit, Run*: John Updike's Criticism of 'The Return to Nature.'" *Twentieth Century Literature* 12 (April 1966): 3–14.

Burchard, Rachael C. *John Updike: Yea Savings.* Carbondale: Southern Illinois University Press, 1971.

Burgess, Anthony. "Language, Myth, and Mr. Updike." *Commonweal* 83 (1966): 557–59.

Callahan, Patrick. "The Poetry of Imperfection." *The Prairie Schooner* 39 (1966): 364–65.

Detweiler, Robert. *John Updike.* New York: Twayne, 1972.

Doner, Dean. "Rabbit Angstrom's Unseen World." *New World Writing* 20 (1962): 58–75.

Doody, Terrence A. "Updike's Idea of Reification." *Contemporary Literature* 20 (1979): 203–20.

Elistratova, A. "Man Is a Tragic Animal: John Updike's Two Novels." *Inostronnaya Literature* 2 (1963): 220–26.

Falk, Wayne. "*Rabbit Redux*: Time/Order/God." *Modern Fiction Studies* 20 (1974): 59–75.

Fisher, Richard E. "John Updike: Theme and Form in the Garden of Epiphanies." *Moderna Sprak* 56 (1962): 225–60.

Flint, Joyce. "John Updike and *Couples*: The WASP's Dilemma." *Research Studies* 36 (1968): 340–47.

Galloway, David D. "The Absurd Man as Saint: The Novels of John Updike." *Modern Fiction Studies* 11 (1964): 111–27.

Gilman, Richard. "A Distinguished Image of Precarious Life." *Commonweal* 73 (1960): 128–29.

Gingher, Robert S. "Has Updike Anything to Say?" *Modern Fiction Studies* 20 (1974): 97–105.

Gordon, J. "Updike Redux" *Ramparts* 10 (1972): 56–59.

Greiner, Donald J. *The Other John Updike: Poems, Short Stories, Prose, Play.* Athens: Ohio University Press, 1981.

Hamilton, Alice, and Kenneth Hamilton. *The Elements of John Updike.* Grand Rapids, Mich.: William B. Eerdmans, 1970.

Harper, Howard M., Jr. *Desperate Faith: A Study of Bellow, Salinger, Mailer, Baldwin, and Updike.* Chapel Hill: University of North Carolina Press, 1967.

Heyen, William. "Sensibilities." *Poetry* 115 (1970): 426–28.

Hicks, Granville. "John Updike." In *Literary Horizons.* New York: New York University Press, 1970.

Hill, John S. "Quest for Belief: Theme in the Novels of John Updike." *Southern Humanities Review* 3 (1969): 166–78.

Hogan, Robert E. "Catharism and John Updike's *Rabbit, Run.*" *Renascence* 32 (1980): 229–39.

Hunt, George W. *John Updike and the Three Great Secret Things: Sex, Religion, and Art.* Grand Rapids, Mich.: William B. Eerdmans, 1980.

Kauffman, Stanley. "Onward with Updike." *The New Republic,* 24 September 1966, 15.

Klinkowitz, Jerome. *Literary Subversions: New American Fiction and the Practice of Criticism.* Carbondale: Southern Illinois University Press, 1984.

Lurie, Alison, "Witches and Fairies: Fitzgerald to Updike." *The New York Review of Books,* 2 December 1971, 6–11.

Lyons, Eugene. "John Updike: The Beginning and the End." *Critique: Studies in Modern Fiction* 14 (1972): 44–59.

Macnaughton, William R., ed. *Critical Essays on John Updike.* Boston: G. K. Hall, 1982.

Mailer, Norman. "Norman Mailer vs. Nine Writers." *Esquire* 60 (1963): 63–69.

Markle, Joyce B. *Fighters and Lovers: Theme in the Novels of John Updike.* New York: New York University Press, 1973.

Mathews, John T. "The Word as Scandal: Updike's *A Month of Sundays.*" *Arizona Quarterly* 39 (1983): 351–80.

Mizener, Arthur. *The Sense of Life in the Modern Novel.* Boston: Houghton Mifflin, 1964.

Myers, David. "The Questing Fear: Christian Allegory in John Updike's *The Centaur.*" *Twentieth Century Literature* 17 (1971): 73–82.

Oates, Joyce Carol. Review of *The Coup,* by John Updike. *The New Republic,* 6 January 1979, 32–35.

Petter, H. "John Updike's Metaphoric Novels." *English Studies* 50 (1969): 197–206.

Podhoretz, Norman. "A Dissent on Updike." In *Doings and Undoings.* New York: Noonday, 1964.

Regan, Robert Alton. "Updike's Symbol of the Center." *Modern Fiction Studies* 20 (1974): 77–96.

Samuels, Charles Thomas. "The Art of Fiction XLIII: John Updike." *The Paris Review*, no. 45 (1968): 85–117.

Strandberg, Victor. "John Updike and the Changing of the Gods." *Mosaic* 12, no. 1 (1978): 157–75.

Stubbs, John C. "The Search for Perfection in *Rabbit, Run.*" *Critique: Studies in Modern Fiction* 10 (1968): 94–101.

Taylor, Larry E. *Pastoral and Anti-Pastoral in John Updike's Fiction.* Carbondale: Southern Illinois University Press, 1971.

Theroux, Paul. Review of *Too Far to Go*, by John Updike. *The New York Times Book Review*, 14 March 1979, 7.

Thorburn, David, and Howard Eiland, eds. *John Updike: A Collection of Critical Essays.* Englewood Cliffs, N.J.: Prentice-Hall, 1979.

Vargo, Edward P. *Rainstorms and Fire: Ritual in the Novels of John Updike.* Port Washington, N.Y.: Kennikat, 1973.

Vickery, John B. "*The Centaur*: Myth, History, and Narrative." *Modern Fiction Studies* 20 (Spring 1974): 29–44.

Ward, John A. "John Updike's Fiction." *Critique: Studies in Modern Fiction* 5 (1962): 27–40.

Waxman, Robert E. "Invitations to Dread: John Updike's Metaphysical Quest." *Renascence* 29 (1977): 201–10.

Wood, Michael. "Great American Fragments." *The New York Review of Books*, 14 December 1972, 12–18.

Wyatt, Bryant N. "John Updike: The Psychological Novel in Search of Structure." *Twentieth Century Literature* 13 (July 1967): 89–96.

Yates, Norris. "The Doubt and Faith of John Updike." *College English Studies* 26 (1965): 469–74.

Youngerman Miller, Miriam. "A Land Too Ripe for Enigma: John Updike as Regionalist." *Arizona Quarterly* 40 (1984): 197–218.

Acknowledgments

"The Private Vice of John Updike" by John W. Aldridge from *Time to Murder and Create: The Contemporary Novel in Crisis* by John W. Aldridge, © 1966 by John W. Aldridge. Reprinted by permission of the author and David McKay Co., Inc.

"John Updike: Style in Search of a Center" by Richard H. Rupp from *Celebration in Postwar American Fiction 1956–1967* by Richard H. Rupp, © 1970 by the University of Miami Press. Reprinted by permission.

"Post-Pill Paradise Lost: John Updike's *Couples*" by David Lodge from *The Novelist at the Crossroads and Other Essays on Fiction and Criticism* by David Lodge, © 1971 by David Lodge. This essay originally appeared in *New Blackfriars* 51, no. 606 (1970). Reprinted by permission of *New Blackfriars*, Oxford, England.

"A Compromised Environment" (originally entitled "A Compromised Environment [John Updike]") by Tony Tanner from *City of Words: American Fiction 1950–1970* by Tony Tanner, © 1971 by Tony Tanner. Reprinted by permission of the author and Harper & Row Publishers.

"Updike's American Comedies" by Joyce Carol Oates from *Modern Fiction Studies* 21, no. 3 (Fall 1975), © 1975 by the Purdue Research Foundation. Reprinted by permission of the Purdue Research Foundation, West Lafayette, Indiana.

"John Updike's Love of 'Dull Bovine Beauty'" by Mary Allen from *The Necessary Blankness: Women in Major American Fiction of the Sixties* by Mary Allen, © 1976 by the Board of Trustees of the University of Illinois. Reprinted by permission of the University of Illinois Press.

"The Novel as Lyric Elegy: The Mode of Updike's *The Centaur*" by James M. Mellard from *Texas Studies in Literature and Language* 21, no. 1 (Spring 1979), © 1979 by the University of Texas Press. Reprinted by permission.

"John Updike: A Literary Spider" by Jane Barnes from *Virginia Quarterly Review* 57, no. 1 (Winter 1981), © 1981 by *Virginia Quarterly Review*. Reprinted by permission.

"Bech, Passing" by Cynthia Ozick from *Art and Ardor* by Cynthia Ozick, © 1983 by Cynthia Ozick. Reprinted by permission of Alfred A. Knopf, Inc., and Raines & Raines.

163

"*The Coup*" by Donald J. Greiner from *John Updike's Novels* by Donald J. Greiner, © 1984 by Donald J. Greiner. Reprinted by permission of the author and Ohio University Press, Athens, Ohio.

Index

165